G000069112

iN GUIDE ROME

When you stroll through Rome you'll be as much aware of the days of its mythical founder, Romulus, as of the rulers of the Roman Empire and the popes who resided and ruled in the capital of Christianity as secular leaders during the Renaissance and Baroque periods. Rome, like no other place in Europe, reveals to you the history of our cultures. Yet it is not only the museums that impress visitors to Rome. In the shadow of the ancient structures there is a vibrant, pulsating modern city. Here you'll find restaurants, bars, stages, squares filled with bustling acitivity and cheerful busyness. Romans live their lives in a way that combines southern joie de vivre and a relaxed attitude; the atmosphere in this city is stimulating and inspiring, yet it is also laid back so you can just drift along. Or just do as Goethe once put it: "The current will carry you along here as soon as you step on board of the ship…"

InGuide Rome is illustrated with the stunning photographs you would expect to find in a large coffee-table book yet it is also a highly informative travel guide. District by district, inspiring images and vivid descriptions introduce all the sights, revealing many amazing facts about the city and its people, about art and culture, about the everyday and the unusual. In "Compact Rome", insider tips point out the best restaurants, hotels, and shops, as well as trendy neighborhoods, important addresses, and useful facts. Another chapter introduces the top museums in detailed descriptions and photographs. Finally, the City Walks are packed with shopping and dining tips that will inspire you to explore all of the Rome districts and areas. A detailed, removable city map completes this unique picture travel guide. It makes it easy for you to find all the city's highlights by grid reference.

CONTENTS

Left: For millennia the Tiber was an important trade route linking Rome with its port at Ostia. Preceding pages: the Pantheon, originally built in the name of all deities, and Castel Sant Angelo, built as a mausoleum.

In the daytime the city's best-known flower market is held at the Campo de' Fiori; at night the square, watched over by the Giardano Bruno monument, turns into a lively and trendy meeting place.

The city was founded on the Palatine Hill, one of the Seven Hills of Rome. Now home to millions, Rome was important even in ancient times, and was one of the founding cities of Western civilization. The hills were first settled in the Iron Age, spreading out to the valleys later on, and over the course of the centuries the "knee", the bend in the River Tiber, was also settled. As the number of people multiplied, so did the buildings. Today the Centro Storico, the historic area around the Piazza del Popolo, the Spanish Steps, the Piazza Venezia, and the bend in the Tiber, forms the heart of the Eternal City "caput mundi" – the capital of the world.

People approaching the city from the north in days gone by would have entered through a gate in the Aurelian Walls, the Porta del Popolo, arriving at the Piazza del Popolo. The "square of the people" we see today is the work of the architect Giuseppe Valadier, who wanted to "open up" Rome. When he started to redesign the piazza in 1816, he left the 1,500-year-old porta standing, as well as the 17th-century twin churches, Santa Maria in Montesanto and Santa Maria dei Miracoli, which flank the entrance to the Via del Corso to the south. On either side of the churches, the Via del

Babuino and the Via di Ripetta lead out at an oblique angle into the very heart of the old city; the layout is known as Il Tridente because the three streets diverge like the prongs of a trident, an ancient weapon used in gladiatorial combat. To the east of the square, steps lead to the Pincio Hill.

On the south side of the Piazza del Popolo are the twin baroque churches of Santa Maria in Montesanto and Santa Maria dei Miracoli (on the right in the large picture; above and top: two interior views). It is not accidental that they resemble a stage setting: Carlo Rainaldi, who built them on the orders of Alexander VII, wanted to impress those who were arriving from the north with this image of perfect symmetry.

The Via di Ripetta leads from the Piazza del Popolo to the Tiber. Today, it is the site of two historic memorials to Augustus, Rome's first emperor: the Ara Pacis, which is dedicated to him, and the mausoleum designed by him. The Ara Pacis, or Altar of Peace, was commissioned by the Senate in 9 BC to celebrate the triumphal return of Augustus and the end of the civil war; it was originally located on the Campus Martius. Over the centuries, parts of the monument became scattered about Italy in various museums and it had to be reconstructed; it was opened to the public in its current location in 1938.

be a tribute to the greatness of the king of France in the heart of Rome. However, the cardinal's idea was not without opposition and initially several popes refused to allow the steps to be built. The nearby Caffè Greco has been popular with book and espresso lovers – for almost 250 years.

Beautifully situated on the Pincio Hill above the Piazza di Spagna, the villa was built in the 16th century on top of the remains of the ancient villa of Lucius Licinius Lucullus, initially by Nanni di Baccio Bigio, and then enlarged by Annibale Lippi on the orders of Cardinal Giovanni Ricci. Designed in the style of a Roman country estate, the estate is named after Cardinal Ferdinando de' Medici, who acquired it in 1576 to house his collection of antiquities. For three years, from 1630 to 1633, Galileo Galilei was imprisoned in the Villa Medici on the orders of the Divine Office. In 1803 Napoleon I

moved the headquarters of a French academy into the Villa Medici; the school had been founded in Rome in 1666 under Louis XIV and was previously based in the Palazzo Salviati on the Corso. Since then, the villa has been home to young scholars – mainly of the visual arts and music.

The villa's garden side is richly decorated with finds from antiquity (large picture). Stunning ceiling frescoes (above) were discovered during the restoration of the "studiolo", Ferdinando de' Medici's study. From the terrace, you can enjoy superb views across the city (top), extending as far as the Castello di St. Angelo, from where Queen Christina of Sweden is said to have fired a canon ball that can still be seen today in the villa's fountain.

The area around Piazza di Spagna – the Via dei Condotti, the Via Borgognona, and part of the Via del Babuino – is a mecca for lovers of high fashion. This is where you will find all the great names in haute couture such as Versace, Gucci, Prada, Armani, Valentino, and Laura Biagiotti. In 2007, Fendi opened a flagship store on the Via Borgognona in a 15th-century villa, where the creations of the top couturier are displayed like works of art in a gallery. The showpiece is a 9-m (29-ft) long chandelier made from precious Murano glass and hanging above the silver staircase. The luxury jeweler Bulgari has a branch at the entrance to the Via dei Condotti, also selling handbags and other accessories. On the Via del Corso, in the Piazza Colonna, there is a branch of the upscale department store chain Rinascente, and the old-established music shop Ricordi has a "mediastore" on this

street. Not quite as exclusive, but well worth a visit, are the shops on the Via Nazionale, the Via del Tritone, and the Via Cola di Rienzo. Stores on the Via del Corso specialize in "young fashion". And if you are interested in antiques, make sure you take a stroll down the Via del Babuino.

From A for Armani to Z for Zegna, and from B for Biblos e Babile to V far Vale – every child in Rome knows the alphabet of the tsars of fashion. Italian fashion is one of the country's chief exports, but inevitably the creations that are displayed like works of art in the city's main shopping avenues come at a price – alas!

The Colonna di Marco Aurelio – the Column of Emperor Marcus Aurelius – was modelled on the Trajan's Column and also depicts theatres of war: the ribbon of reliefs made from 29 Carrara marble drums and which wind their way around the column illustrate the emperor's victorious campaigns against the Marcomanni and the Sarmatians. Nearly 30 m tall (98 ft), and, including the base, reaching a height of 42 m (137 ft), the column was built in the 2nd century. In the 16th century the statue of the emperor was replaced by a bronze figure of the Apostle Paulus, created by Domenico

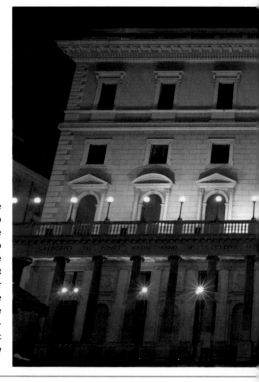

A staircase leads up the inside of the Colonna di Marco Aurelio (top right), standing in the middle of the Piazza Colonna, to the top of the column. A plaque on the Palazzo Wedekind, built in 1838 for the German banker Karl Wedekind, tells us that the *Il Tempo* newspaper was once based here. The remarkable portico (large picture) has 16 Ionic columns that came originally from ancient Veji.

Fontana. A fountain designed by Giacomo della Porta is in front of the column. On the north side of the piazza, named after the column, is the Palazzo Chigi, begun in 1562 by Giacomo della Porta and completed by Carlo Maderno; it is the official residence of the Italian prime minister.

In Rome there is a fountain on almost every street corner and in almost every square – there are several hundred of them, perhaps even a thousand, and they are all a delight for the eye. And not only for the eye: the simplest kind consists of a bent metal outflow pipe, generally with a small basin beneath it. Passers-by can stop to quench their thirst at these nose-shaped pipes, which the Romans have affectionately nicknamed nasoni (big noses). The large, elaborate, and artistically significant fountains are an indirect legacy of ancient times. They originated in the fountains that grew up at the sites of ancient shrines once dedicated to water spirits (nymphaea), at the ends of the aqueducts that transported drinking water into the city from the mountains many hundreds of miles away. Three of these aqueducts are still intact and continue to supply the fountains that the popes had

built in the places where the pagan nymphs were said to have lived: the Aqua Virgo supplies the world-famous baroque Trevi Fountain; the Aqua Claudia supplies the Moses Fountain in the Piazza San Bernardo; and the Aqua Augusta ends in the waterfalls by the Villa Aldobrandini in Frascati.

There are "celebrities" among the fountains in Rome, too: the most famous is the Fontana di Trevi; closely following are the Fontana dei Quattro Fiumi (large picture: Bernini's statue of the River Ganges in the Four-Rivers-Fountain) on the Piazza Navona and the fountain on the Piazza della Rotonda (top). However, many of the lesser-known fountains (above) in the city's streets are also decorated with beautiful sculptures and mosaics.

Rome's largest and most celebrated fountain is the Fontana di Trevi. It was built in 1732 in front of the Palazzo Poli to the designs of Nicola Salvi as a receptacle for the Acqua Virgo, which had existed since ancient times. The name Trevi probably refers to an earlier and much more modest fountain dating from the 15th century, which stood at the junction of three roads ("tre vie"). Plans to replace the old fountain with a new one had been around for a while, when Pope Clemens XII launched a competition for the design of the new fountain, which was won by Salvi. However, the roughly

26-m-tall (85 ft) fountain could only be built across the entire length of the square when the pope decided to make use of the entire façade of the ducal palace as a backdrop, despite the bitter protests of the Duke of Poli. The fountain was inaugurated in 1744, even before its completion in 1762.

The Duke of Poli was none too happy that the back wall of his only recently built palace was to serve as a stage set (large picture) for the Fontana di Trevi. The fountain dominates the entire Piazza Trevi (top). The central group of figures (above), created by Pietro Bracci after 1759, depicts the "realm of the oceans". It has become a tradition to throw a coin into the fountain to guarantee that one day you'll return here.

Italy is a fairly young republic: on June 26,1946, a narrow majority of the country's voting population decided in a referendum to abolish the monarchy. The church had pleaded for its retention; anything else would be a dangerous gamble. Umberto II, the last king of Italy, went into exile. In order to house the various committees and organs of the new state no new buildings were erected in Rome – for conservationist reasons too – but instead several centuries-old "palazzi" were chosen. The Quirinal Palace was selected as the residence of the new "first man", the president of the republic. Built in the 16th century as a papal summer palace, and converted into a residence for Italy's monarch in 1870, the palace is the largest Renaissance building of its kind in the world. The Palazzo Chigi became the seat of the prime minister and his staff, while the Chamber of Deputies meets at the Palazzo

Montecitorio. The Senate is based in the Palazzo Madama. Although at times the politicians have been heard to complain about the antiquated conditions inside these magnificent old palaces, they still feel rather comfortable here on the whole, even the Socialists and Communists!

Generally referred top just as "Quirinale", the Palazzo del Quirinale (Top: an overall view; above: the palace guard; large picture: the Sala degli Ambasciatori) today serves as the presidential palace. It is located on the Quirinal Hill – one of the legendary seven hills of Rome – and is open to the public only on Sunday mornings.

Maffeo Barberini was born into an influential family of merchants in Florence. During his time in office as Pope Urban VIII (1623–1644) he was lucky enough to be able to call on the genius of two of the most important architects of the Baroque: Borromini and Bernini. Soon after he had been chosen as the new pope he decided to have a magnificent palace built for his family. Initially under the direction of the architect Carlo Maderno, a palace was built on the Via delle Quattro Fontane that was remarkable in art historical terms because its ground plan was not the defensively enclosed rectangular

Allegory of Divine Providence and Barberini Power is the title of Pietro da Cortona's ceiling fresco (large picture) decorating the two-floor high "gran salone" of the Palazzo Barberini. It glorifies Pope Urban VIII and his family. The three bees are a reference to the Barberini family's coat of arms. Today the palace (above: Borromini's helicoidal stairs) houses part of the collection of the Galleria Nazionale d'Arte Antica (top right).

shape that had hitherto been the norm for city palaces: with its central structure and two advancing side wings it resembled instead a large country villa. After Maderno's death in 1629 Bernini continued its construction; previously Borromini had already been Maderno's most important co-worker.

The church was built during the reign of Nicholas III (pope 1277–1280) on the site of a temple that had erroneously been attributed to Minerva, the Roman goddess of wisdom, hence the name. In reality the church, begun by the two Dominican monks Fra Sisto Fiorentino and Fra Ristoro da Campi and completed in 1370 Church of St. Mary, the only Gothic church in Rome, stands on the remains of an ancient sanctuary of Isis; although this was accidental it is still remarkable because the Christian veneration of Mary had an iconographic precursor in the cult of Isis in Ancient

Egypt (in the depiction of a mother and her child). Characteristic of the church is a mix of styles – designed initially as a Renaissance structure, remodeled later in the Baroque period, and finally "re-Goth-icized" in the 19th century. Visiting the church is a stroll through Italian art history.

Santa Maria sopra Minerva is a three-aisled basilica church with cross-ribbed vaulting built on a T-shaped ground plan. The vaults were not painted until the middle of the 19th century and the pillars were then clad in imitation marble (large picture).

Under the high altar lie the mortal remains of Saint Catharine of Siena (top). To the left of the altar stands Michelangelo's famous statue of *Christ the Redeemer* (above).

West of the Via del Corso, on the Piazza della Rotonda, stands one of the most impressive buildings of ancient times: the Pantheon. As its Greek name implies, the Pantheon was a temple dedicated to the gods. The free-standing centrally planned structure on a circular ground plan, with a mighty dome and gabled atrium has dominated this squarefor more than 1,800 years. A baroque fountain created by Giacomo della Porta in 1578 stands in front of the Pantheon. In 1711 an Egyptian obelisk of a nearby Isis sanctuary, excavated at the church of Sant'Ignazio di Loyola, was placed on its

plinth, which is also decorated with dolphin motifs and the insignia of Clement XI (pope 1700–1721). The obelisk was originally erected in Heliopolis during the reign of Rameses II. The piazza is one of the favorite meeting places in the heart of the Centro Storico for the locals as well as tourists.

All around the Rotonda, as the Romans say when referring to the Piazza della Rotonda, there's always something going on (large picture and top; above: a view from the Pantheon's tympanum toward the fountain and its obelisk). Customers are served in the cafés and restaurants until very late into the night.

West of the Via del Corso, on the Piazza della Rotonda, is one of the most impressive buildings of ancient times: the Pantheon, as its Greek name reveals, was a temple dedicated to all the gods. The dome has the same diameter as height (43.4 m/142 ft). First built in 27 BC, the Pantheon was destroyed by fire in AD 80 and reconstructed during the reign of Emperor Hadrian (117–138). In the 5th century, the "pagan" place of worship was closed, but Pope Boniface IV prevented its destruction and converted it into a Christian church. The round opening in the dome, the *oculus* (eye),

The Pantheon is one of the greatest domed buildings. Its interior is arched over by a hemispherical dome with a waffle-slab ceiling (large picture), whereas the walls are structured by niches and columns (above). The inscription on the portico reads "M(ARCUS) AGRIPPA L(UCII) F(ILIUS) CO(N)S(UL) TERTIUM FECIT" (top right), which means that "Marcus Agrippa, the son of Lucius, during his third consulate, built this".

was believed to have had mystical significance, creating a link to the world of the gods. Used as a mausoleum from the time of the Renaissance, the tombs of the painter Raphael (d. 1520) and the last resting place of Victor Emmanuel II (d. 1878), the first king of a unified Italy, are found here.

The ancient Romans recognized many deities and adopted foreign gods, such as the Egyptian goddess, Isis. Up until the 5th century BC, the Roman gods were personifications of nature; then, under the influence of the Etruscans, they also accepted but renamed the Greek gods. Zeus and Hera, a couple who had many rows because of the numerous amorous escapades of the Father of Gods, became Jupiter, responsible for thunder and lightening, and Juno, in charge of families and birth. The ten other chief Roman gods, the "Olympians", and their areas of responsibility were: Apollo (poetry), Ceres (fertility), Diana (the hunt), Mars (war), Minerva (wisdom), Venus (love), Neptune (the sea), Vesta (the hearth and its fire), and Vulcan (fire and metal working); Mercury was the messenger of the gods, as well as the god of thieves and merchants. Other gods were added to the 12 main ones, including Bacchus, the

God of wine, and Pluto, the lord of the underworld. Officially, they ceased to exist in Christian times; their temples were closed or, like the Pantheon, converted into churches. However, the old gods lived on in art and literature, and continue to enrich our lives to this day.

The frescoes created by Raphael and his pupils in 1518 for the Villa Farnesina portray the myth of Cupid and Psyche – including the Council of the Gods (large picture). Above: Guido Reni's fresco (1612–14) in the central hall of the Casino Rospigliosi-Pallavicini in Rome shows Apollo pursuing Aurora, the goddess of the dawn, in his chariot.

The palace was built in the 16th century for the Medci family as a city residence on the present Corso Rinascimento, not far from the Piazza Navona. It was named after "Madama" Margaret of Parma, the illegitimate daughter of Emperor Charles V and the Flemish farm woman Johanna van der Gheynst, who lived here from 1559 to 1567. Unlike his numerous other illegitimate children, Charles recognized Margaret as his "natural" daughter. In 1536, the then fourteen-year-old girl was married to the Duke Alessandro de' Medici; and on her second marriage in 1538 to Ottavio Farnese, the Duke of Parma and Piacenza.

In 1559 Philip II of Spain made her the regent of the Netherlands. The baroque façade of the palace was only added in the 17th century. From 1871, after the collapse of the monarchy, the Palazzo has been the seat of the Senate, one of the two chambers of the Italian parliament.

Two future popes, Giovanni de' Medici (Leo X) and Giulio de' Medici (Clement VII) lived at this palace (top: the southern side), before "Madama" Margaret of Parma, the widow of Alessandro de' Medici, moved in. Large picture: the magnificent stucco frescoes in the Sala Maccari illustrate episodes from the history of the Senate in Antiquity. Above: the Senate sits today in the large auditorium furnished as an assembly hall.

This piazza was not "laid out", it evolved into its present form over several centuries in an organic way. Its elongated shape indicates that it was once a stadium, built by Caesar and expanded in the year 85 under Domitian. In the early Middle Ages, a church was built on the site where St Agnes had suffered a martyr's death; living quarters and shops were constructed under the former spectator stands, which gradually developed into larger buildings. In 1477, Sixtus IV granted permission for a market and horse races were held until 1495, when it was paved. In the 17th and 18th centuries, the piazza was

To finance the Fontana dei Quattro Fiumi, the Fountain of the Four Rivers, special taxes were raised in 1651, including a tax on bread – which was not a popular move. Large picture: Bernini's *Allegory of the Ganges*. Above: the Fountain of Neptune on the north side of the square was decorated with sculptures by Antonio della Bitta and Gregorio Zappalà in the second half of the 19th century. Top right: local artists display their work.

flooded and turned into a lake during the celebrations held by the powerful Pamphili family. In the mid-17th century, two rival architects were commissioned to improve the square: Gianlorenzo Bernini created the Fountain of the Four Rivers, and Francesco Borromini rebuilt the church, Sant'Agnese in Agone.

This church, dedicated to French King Louis IX who was canonized in 1297, is a place of worship for French residents in Rome – the coat of arms on the gable features lilies, the emblem of France. There are figures from French history on the façade including Charlemagne, St Jeanne de Valois, and St Clotilde. Construction of the three-aisled pillar basilica began in 1518 and after a lengthy interruption was completed in 1589, with the aid of financial contributions from the French king. A side chapel contains three large paintings by Caravaggio (1571–1610), showing scenes from the life of

The three paintings produced by Caravaggio for the Contarelli chapel in the church of San Luigi dei Francesi depict *The Calling of St Matthew* (top right), *The Inspiration of St Matthew* (above), and *The Martyrdom of St Matthew* (large picture). They replace three other painting created ten years previously by the then only 17-year-old artist; their realism was disturbing for many.

the apostle Matthew: his calling, his meeting with the angel, and his martyrdom. Caravaggio is considered the first of the great baroque painters and a master in the use of dramatic lighting; he is well known for his chiaroscuro ("light-dark") painting and strong realism, which shines through his work.

The Campo de' Fiori – now the seting for a flower and food market – is a rectangular-shaped piazza that was once used for horse racing and executions – there was a permanent gallows on the spot. The best-known offender put to death here was philosopher Giordano Bruno, who died at the stake on 17 February 1600. He was accused of heresy as, among other things, he was a proponent of heliocentrism, publicly doubting that the earth was the focal point of the universe. A memorial to him was erected in 1884, a gift of the Freemasons in a sign of protest against the Church: Pope Leo

The lively market in the Campo de' Fiori still retains the bustling air of the medieval inns that once flourished here. Even if you don't wish to buy any flowers, fruit, vegetables, or bread, you'll enjoy watching the lively scenes from one of the street cafés: a strong espresso in front of you, the endless sky above you – and many Italians glued to their mobile phones next to you.

XII had accused the members of this order of being "destroyers of the faith". At odds with its dark past, its name means "field of flowers", from the time when the area was just a meadow. During the day, flowers and local food are sold, and in the evening, the young people of Rome congregate here.

Rome has been a city of pilgrimages since time immemorial. Some come because of their faith, others immerse themselves in beautiful architecture, and others just appreciate the city's magic. It is easiest to feel this magic if you allow yourself to join the local Romans on their evening strolls through the city. An excellent starting point is the Spanish Steps, from where you can visit Giolitti's, Rome's most famous ice-cream parlor which opened in 1890, and located just behind the Chamber of Deputies, on the Palazzo Montecitorio where crowds converge between 22.00 and midnight. Ice-cream cones in hand, the nocturnal pilgrims continue toward the Pantheon, where you can sip an outrageously expensive latte in one of the street cafés or drink a much better one at half the price while standing on the Piazza di Sant' Eustachio. Thus fortified you'll continue to the Piazza Navona, of which it is said that

it is too beautiful to allow for anyone to show off in the face of its competition. Nevertheless, even the Romans who are usually very interested in showing off, love the square above anything and hang around here for many hourse before finally finishing their nighttime stroll at the nearby Campo de' Fiori.

The mottos for a night in Rome are twofold: see and be seen, as well as live and let live. Although they are true in the daytime too, the night belongs to the Romans themselves – to the night owls, who travel from their home on the outskirts of the city to pay homage to the "struscio", the traditional nighttime strolling through the city.

The Piazza Farnese is graced by two beautiful fountains, designed by Girolamo Rainaldi 1626. They were made from reused granite bathtubs which were unearthed from the Caracalla thermae, and the lilies that were later attached to the fountains indicate the coat of arms of the Farnese family, after whom the square and the palace that dominates it were named. The palace was built between 1514 and 1580 on the orders of the then cardinal Alessandro Farnese, the future Pope Paul III. One of the most impressive Renaissance palaces in the city, its construction was started by Antonio da Sangallo

the Younger, and was continued after his death by Michelange-lo. Following his death, work on the palace was eventually completed by Giacomo della Porta who designed the back of the building. In 1635 the French government moved its embassy into the palace and is still based there today.

The fountains on the Farnese (large picture) are another perfect meeting place for young Romans. The square is a beautiful backdrop to the many restaurants (above) in the square. Top: the lavish detail reveals the attention that was given to the design of all the houses lining the Piazza Farnese.

In order to protect both people and monuments from exhaust fumes, the Centro Storico has been declared a "blue zone", banned to private traffic. However, many Romans seem to know someone whose brother, sister, uncle, or aunt works for the authorities – and over 40,000 exceptions have been granted. As an outsider, driving a car in Rome is a risky business. Romans, like Italians in general, are good at communicating with their hands, even when driving, so foreign motorists in Rome also need to be able to decipher even the most casual hand signals – a red traffic light seems to be a mere recommendation to stop. Watch out for flashing headlights, which, rather than "after you" often mean "after me", while the horn is used extravagantly by all drivers to warn others of their presence. Visitors are advised to explore on foot or use public transport. There are only two lines on the

underground rail system, the Metropolitana, but there are numerous taxis: licensed taxis are white or yellow and have a number; avoid the unlicensed ones. If you really want to venture out onto the roads, you can rent a scooter. This allows you to weave in and out between the cars and park easily.

Foreigners are expressly warned against taking a car onto the streets of the eternally jammed city. It is rarely a pleasure even on a bike or a scooter – there are simply too many cars and too little space.

Rome 51

Jewish merchants had settled in Rome even before the birth of Christ. For a long time they were spared any repressive measures, but in 1555 the Jewish community was forced by Paul IV (pope 1555–1559) to resettle in an area on the banks of the River Tiber that was considered particularly un-healthy. Only during the day time were they allowed to leave this ghetto that was sur-rounded by a high wall. They also had to resign themselves to the fact that certain profes-sions were barred to them and every Sunday they were forced to listen to a Christian sermon. The Catholic Church did not

abandon this humiliation until 1848 when Pius IX (pope 1846–1878) freed them from the ghetto. Jews were still deprived of the full citizens' right until the pope was stripped of his secular power over Rome in 1870. One of the first moves of the government was to order the demolition of the wall.

Picturesque courtyards and restaurants today define the area around the Via del Portico d'Ottavia in the heart of the former ghetto. In a district of less than one hectare (about 2 acres) several thousand people who belonged to the oldest Jewish community in Europe were crowded together in a dreary, sad corner of Rome, separated from Trastevere by the River Tiber.

The "Societas Jesu", the society of Jesus, was founded in 1534 by the Spanish nobleman Ignatius von Loyola (1491–1556). A spiritual community, it differed from all previously existing religious orders in that its members did not live in monastic seclusion, but worked in the world at large. In 1540 Paul III (pope 1534–1549) approved the society. The Jesuits quickly grew in importance and became the most influential order of the Counter reformation, supported by those who were loyal to the pope. In accordance with their new standing they wanted to convert a small chapel as their

The high baroque decoration of the church, begun in 1568, was only added some hundred years after its completion in 1582. Langhaus Giovanni Battista Gaulli, "Baciccia", created the *Worship of the Holy Name of Jesus* ceiling fresco between 1668 to 1683 (large picture). The interior of the church (above and top right) is designed to allow the altar to be viewed from all angles.

headquarters in Rome. Alessandro Farnese (1520–1589), the grandson of the Farnese pope Paul III, who was made a cardinal in 1534, and a cardinal deacon in 1580, decided that Giacomo Barozzi da Vignola should be the architect of the project and he also financed much of the church.

If someone shouted the slogan "Viva Verdi!" in the mid-19th century in Italy, he or she was not cheering the well-known opera composer but Victor Emmanuel II, who had ruled the kingdom of Piedmont-Sardinia since 1849. Many Italians wanted him to be the king of a united Italy. The name "Verdi" was made up of the initial letters of the title that the monarch would be granted on ascending the throne: Vittorio Emanuele Re d'Italia. In 1861, the supporters of a united Italy finally had their wish and Victor Emmanuel became king of Italy. Born in 1820, he had taken part in the First Italian

The vast complex on the Piazza Venezia, made from shiny white limestone, is colloquially given derogatory nicknames by locals such as "typewriter" or "wedding cake". The building, regarded as too large and too pompous by most Romans, was not inaugurated until 1911, after 26 years of construction.

War of Independence with his father, Charles Albert of Sardinia, and had also been joint leader of the Risorgimento (the movement for unification) with the freedom fighter Garibaldi. The king was much loved by his people – though this love did not extend to his memorial, designed by Giuseppe Sacconi.

In the beginning, there was only a marshy valley where people used to bury their dead. Once the surrounding hills were settled the valley became the heart of ancient Rome: the Forum Romanum.

The 20th-century Roman writer Alberto Moravia described Rome as a city that has many more monuments than houses. People were already concerned about protecting this unique legacy as far back as 458, when the Western Roman Emperor Majorian ordered that "everything that contributes to the brilliance of the city should be maintained in good order by the zeal of the citizens". With its many splendid churches and monuments, Rome's antiquities are its greatest attraction, drawing millions every year. Many visitors are astounded by the wealth of ancient remains, which can feel like being in open-air museum.

According to legend, the Trojan Prince Aeneas, son of a king and the goddess Aphrodite, fled from the burning city of Troy and was washed across the sea to the Italian coast, together with a group of faithful followers. In the Alban Hills (south of Rome) he founded the village of Alba Longa, which became the "mother city" of Rome as the birthplace of the legendary twins: Romulus and Remus. Their Uncle Amulius had seized the throne of Alba Longa, and because the twins were claim it for themselves, they were abandoned in the hills as newborn babies, suckled by a she-wolf, and raised by a shepherd. When they were young men, they decided to found a city of their own. Romulus climbed the hill that is today known as Palatine, while Remus asended the Aventine hill. Whoever spotted more birds, they agreed, should reign over the new town. Romulus won, but

Large picture: The Capitoline Wolf has now been suckling Romulus and Remus for many centuries. For a long time this superb sculpture, which is kept in the Capitoline Museums, was thought to be the work of Etruscans; recent research, however, seems to suggest that it was made until the Middle Ages. Top right: Giuseppe Cesari also illustrated the founding myth of the city in a 16th-century painting.

his brother did not accept defeat. Remus mocked him and jumped over the newly built walls and in return Remulus killed him with the words, "So perish every one that shall hereafter leap over my wall". Romulus then went on to become king of the town, which he named Rome, after himself.

ATVS·POPVLVSQVE·ROMANVS
VMENTA·MARMOREA·MAGISTRATVVM
MPHORVMQVE·AB·VRBE·CONDITA·AD
PORA·DIVI·AVGVSTI·RVDERIBVS
RO·EGESTIS·ERVTA·IMPENSA·ALEX
ESI·CARD·PAVLI·III·PONT·MAX·NEPOT

In ancient times, around the 6th century BC, a temple was dedicated to Jupiter, the most important of the gods, on the top of the Capitol. It could be reached along a winding path from the Forum to the south-east. Today you can climb to the top from the west, up a flight of steps designed by Michelangelo, alongside which runs an older staircase leading to the church of Santa Maria in Aracoeli. Once at the top – it is the lowest of the seven hills of Rome – you are in the heart of a piazza with paving laid out in a geometric pattern, also the work of Michelangelo. In the middle is the equestrian statue

Michelangelo's Piazza del Campidoglio on the Capitol (top right), once the heart of the Roman world, is graced by copy of the equestrian statue of the stoic philosopher and emperor Marcus Aurelius (large picture). The original is now in the Capitoline Museums.

of Marcus Aurelius, the only ancient equestrian bronze to have escaped being melted down in the medieval period because it was thought that the rider was Constantine I, the first Christian Roman emperor. The Palazzo Senatorio on the piazza is today the seat of the mayor of the city of Rome.

Two of the buildings in the square on top of the Capitol – the Palazzo dei Conservatori and the Palazzo Nuovo – are home to the Capitoline Museums. The collection is based on ancient sculptures collected by Sixtus IV (pope 1471–1481) and opened to the public in 1471. The best-known exhibit is the Capitoline Wolf, a bronze statue of the famous wolf who, according to legend, suckled the twins Romulus and Remus. The two human figures are believed to be a later addition. The wolf herself was thought to be an Etruscan work, until the archaeologist and restorer Anna Maria Carruba discovered that the statue was probably created some 1,500 years later. In ancient times large bronze statues were cast as individual pieces and then welded together; however, there are no such welding seams to be found on the Lupa Romana. Another famous piece is the *Thorn-Puller*, a statue of a

boy removing a thorn from his foot, and the *Capitoline Venus* (both 1st century BC) as well as the *Dying Gaul* (the Roman copy of a Greek original that was probably created around circa 220 BC). The Capitoline's Pinacoteca (picture gallery) contains exhibits predominately from the 16th and 17th centuries.

The world's first public museum: in 1734 Clement XII (pope 1730–1740) declared the Palazzo Nuovo built in the previous century a museum. Among its ancient highlights are the remains of a colossal statue of Emperor Constantine I (large picture), the legendary *Thorn-puller* (above) and the equally famous *Dying Gaul* (top).

"Now I'll show you the place in the city where / Any person is most easily found, / So that you do not have to spend much time running about when you / Want to meet him, whether he's a rogue, or whether he's an honest man", wrote the poet Plautus (250–184 BC). He was speaking of the Roman Forum (Forum Romanum) – the complex of squares and buildings (built from the 6th century BC) situated between the Palatine Hill and the Capitol. It was here that religious ceremonies and political meetings took place, speeches were made, and goods were sold. The Roman Forum was always

a major meeting place for Romans throughout history – to discuss business, meet friends, or just while away the hours. With the collapse of the Roman Empire, the buildings were allowed to fall into disrepair. In the Middle Ages, the square was known as Campo Vaccino, the cow pasture.

The Roman Forum was the heart of ancient Rome. Today the ruins of imperial monuments attest to the transient nature of secular power (top). Large picture: the triumphal Arch of Septimius Severus, the Temple of Saturn and the Temple of Vespasian and Titus, with the baroque church Santi Luca e Martina in the background.

In a conscious effort to dissociate themselves from the pagan cult of the gods, the early Christians rejected any visual representation of their beliefs. The same is true for the sacred spaces: for the early Church, God's temple on earth was still the congregation (ecclesia), not the local church. Only in the 3rd century, when it was recognized that images were capable of giving symbolic support to beliefs that have been passed on orally, the Christian appreciation of art took a more positive turn. At the same time the idea of the "hallowing" of the place of worship became prevalent – the theological basis for a Christian architecture that was fundamentally different from that of the distant past: unlike the temples in ancient times, the Christian church was not built to serve simply as a house of God but was also to be a place of assembly for the congregation – that is, it should

FROM ANCIENT TEMPLE TO CHRISTIAN CHURCH

unite both priests and the faithful in front of the altar. Nevertheless, early Christian church architecture continued to make use of ancient building traditions and styles for centuries. Both secular as well as ecclesiastical architectural influences were soon used in church design

Nowhere else can the development from ancient temple to Christian church be observed more clearly than in Rome. Top: a view across the Forum Romanum to the Coliseum; large picture: the Temple of Antonius Pius and Faustina, built in 141 and transformed into the church of San Lorenzo in Miranda in 1150; above: San Giovanni in Laterano – probably the earliest Roman church (4th century).

Gaius Julius Caesar (100–44 BC) was one of the most famous generals and statesmen in the history of the world; he is also known as a chronicler of history and introduced the Julian calendar, the precurser to the Gregorian calendar of today. He used the authority he gained for his campaign victories to form a strategic "triumvirate" together with the wealthy Marcus Licinius Crassus and the general Gnaeus Pompeius Magnus, or Pompey the Great, and this enabled him to be elected a consul in 59 BC. He subjugated the Gaul and led campaigns against Germania and Britannia. Although it was forbidden to the Roman army, Caesar led his troops across the Rubicon in 49 BC, igniting civil war. For five years Caesar fought in almost all Mediterranean countries against Pompey, who had been commissioned by the Senate, until he was able to defeat his troops – and

have Pompey killed. At the height of his powers, in 44 BC, Caesar elected himself dictator for life. The Roman Republic ended soon after he was murdered by his senators.. His successor Augustus deified Caesar as "Divus Iulius" and introduced the title of "caesar" meaning emperor or tasar.

An estimated fifty to sixty Roman senators conspired in the assassination of Caesar under the leadership of Brutus and Cassius (large picture: oil painting by Friedrich Heinrich Füger, 1815; above: a green basalt bust dating from the 1st century). The emperor financed the construction of Forum Julianum or Caesar Forum (top), begun in 54 BC with the spoils of the war against the Gaul.

By the end of the republican era, and in spite of the various civil wars that had taken place over 60 years, the population of Rome had grown so greatly, that the Forum, then about 500 years old, was no longer large enough. Caesar carried out an initial expansion in 54 BC. Around 50 years later, when the population was almost one million, Emperor Augustus (originally Gaius Octavius, 63 BC–AD 14), who was adopted by his great-uncle Caesar and appointed his main heir, carried out a second expansion. In AD 97, under Emperor Nerva (Marcus Cocceius, 30–98) the square in front of a temple to

Augustus could not honor his vows and inaugurate his forum until 40 years after Caesar's murderers, Brutus and Cassius, had died in the Battle of the Philippi. It is conceived as a spacious square flanked by columned walks and side recesses (top right). Everything was dominated by the Temple of Mars Ultor (on the large picture the steps leading up to the podium temple can still be seen). Above: the emperor's statue on the Forum.

Minerva was added. Final expansion took place under Emperor Trajan, who ruled between 98 and 117. A 38-m (124-ft) high column was erected in the forum named after him; its spiral relief celebrates his two victorious campaigns against the Dacians, but most of the carving depicts the Roman army.

The Roman Empire achieved its greatest extent under Emperor Trajan (originally Marcus Ulpius Traianus, 53–117): in 106 the provinces of Dacia (in the area of present-day Romania) and Arabia Petraea (the kingdom of the Nabataeans) were annexed; in the Parthian War (114–117) the provinces of Armenia, Assyria, and Mesopotamia were added. With the spoils from his wars, Trajan financed the construction of the imperial Forum named after him. Almost 80,000 cu m (267,500 cu ft) of soil had to be shifted between 107 and 113 to establish the forum, designed by the architect Apollo-

doros of Damascus. The height of the Column of Trajan marked the height of the soil that had been removed for the Forum. The emperor's ashes were kept in a golden urn in the base. The emporer's statue on top of the column was replaced by Sixtus V (pope 1585–1590) with a statue of St Peter.

The Forum of Trajan is the last, largest and best-preserved imperial forum in the city (large picture). Above: only few ruins remain of the Basilica Ulpia, the largest basilica ever built in Rome and also part of the Forum. Top: one of the relief plaques on the Column of Trajan, created from 17 blocks of marble in 113. It depicts the campaign of the imperial army against the Dacians.

No one knows exactly what happened in the early morning hours of 19 July 64. It is likely that the fire started on the north side of the Circus Maximus. Somewhere between the wooden stalls and small inns, a spark blazed. Flames flared up, and soon they were carried by the strong south-east wind through Rome's narrow alleyways where the wood and straw houses burned like tinder. The fire could not be extinguished, it is said, until six days later, and when the last clouds of smoke had dissipated a picture of unspeakable horror unfolded: two-thirds of the city had burned down, some 200,000 people had lost their homes in the interred narrow alleys – it is not known how many people had died. Among those who had survived, however a rumor soon spread that it had been the Emperor Nero himself who had started the fire; he was said to want to build a new Rome on the rub-

Born Lucius Domitius Ahenobarbus in 37 and renamed after adoption by Claudius in 50 (above: a bust), Nero Claudius Caesar ascended the throne aged 17 years. However, he saw himself as more of an artist. The life of the emperor, who died in 68, still inspired many historical paintings in the 19th and 20th centuries (large picture: a painting by Ulpiano Checa Sanz; top right: the burning of Rome on a publicity postcard).

NERO AND THE BURNING OF ROME

ble of the old, which he would call Neropolis. In order to avert any such suspicions — which according to research carried out more recently were probably unfounded — Nero directed the suspicion of arson to the then still small community of Christians, whom he demanded be brutally pursued.

Where the ruins of the largest amphitheater in history stand, there was once an earlier wooden building erected by Emperor Nero – the stage fell victim to the great fire in the year 64. When Nero had plans drawn for its replacement, he incorporated an artificial pond within the building. In around 72, his successor Vespasian commissioned the three-storey arena. Construction was partially financed by the gold and treasure that had fallen into the hands of the Romans when they plundered the temple at Jerusalem. The games which mark the opening of the Coliseum lasted 100 days, during

"As long as the Coliseum stands, Rome shall stand; when the Coliseum falls, Rome will fall; when Rome falls, the world will fall", said the English Benedictine monk, the Venerable Bede in the 7th century. So there are good reasons not to seal the fate of the building with a "thumbs down" (above). The amphitheater is elliptical in shape, 188 m (617 ft) long and 150 m (492 ft) wide; the façade is 50 m (164 ft) high (large picture, top and right).

which large numbers of people and thousands of animals were killed for the amusement of the baying crowds. The poet Martial (40–102) paid tribute to the emperor Vespasian with the following lines: "Rome has returned to its people, and under your government, Emperor, people are being entertained".

The custom of erecting a triumphal arch for victorious commanders was introduced to Rome by the Etruscan kings. One of the greatest memorials of this type stands near the Coliseum: the Arch of Constantine was erected to the Emperor Constantine I (306–337, (whose real name was Flavius Valerius Constantinus, known as the Great) by the Senate in AD 315 – three years after the emperor's victory over his rivals. The Arch of Constantine is richly decorated with sculptures, its reliefs and statues glorifying the exploits of the emperor on the battlefield. Some of the structural ele-

Although Constantine attributed his victory over co-emperor Maxentius at the Milvian Bridge in 312 to a vision of Christ, his triumphal arch does not display any Christian iconography (large picture; top right a detail of the arch at the top, decorated with reliefs and statues).

ments were stolen from memorials dedicated to former Roman rulers: the statues of four prisoners on the north side of the arch, for example, came from a memorial to Emperor Trajan; the reliefs below were taken from a memorial to Marcus Aurelius. Reliefs inside the arch tell of Trajan's victory over the Dacians.

The Palatine Hill, the legendary site of the foundation of the city, bears the oldest traces of human settlement in Rome, dating back to the 10th century BC. Of the seven classic hills of the city, this was where the rich and famous of ancient times built their lavish residences, including the states-man and great orator Cicero settled and the poet Catullus. The Palatine Hill was also the home of Emperor Augustus and his wife Livia. Later emperors, such as Tiberius, Caligula, and Domitian lived a much more luxurious lifestyle in magnificently designed palaces on the hill. Domitian built

THE PALATINE HILL 26

the Domus Flavia for state purposes and the Domus Augustus as a private palace. But these have not survived. The remains of the former residence of the emperor Tiberius, for example, are now covered by the Farnese Gardens, which were originally laid out in the 16th century.

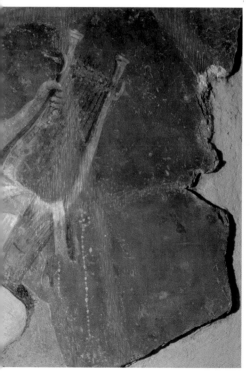

Fresco in the home of Augustus (large picture, c. 30 BC) and painted terracotta reliefs from the Temple of Apollo (above, c. 36 BC) once embellished the palaces on the Palatine Hill. The Farnese pavilions on the Palatine (top) were built in the 16th century for a large private garden.

Four temples from the republican, pre-empire era, some of the oldest structures in the city, are to be found in this former *area sacra* (holy area) as well as the remains of the "Teatro di Pompey". The oldest temple, dedicated to Feronia – revered as the protecting goddess of all freed slaves and the guardian of the springs in the city – is thought to have been constructed in around 300 BC. Another temple was probably built to celebrate the victory over the Carthaginians in 241 BC. The square is part of the Campus Martius (The Field of Mars), an area of publicly owned land used as a place of

public assembly and for military parades. Today it's called Largo the Cat's Forum, because of the large numbers of cats who live around the ruins. In 2001 the cat population in the old town was recognized as a "biocultural legacy" – *i gatti* enjoy special protection in Rome and are cared for by volunteers.

The square was named either after a tower that stood near the house of Johannes Burckhardt, a papal master of ceremonies (*argentoratum* in Latin) who had come to Rome from Strasbourg in the 16th century and lived nearby. Or it might have been named after the silversmiths' shops in the area (*argentarii*). As it is uncertain to whom the four letters in the temple in the 1920s are dedicated to, they are known as A to D.

Several temples had to be demolished to make way for this theater on the ancient Campus Martius (Field of Mars). Originally planned by Julius Caesar, it was completed by Emperor Augustus, who named the building after his sister's son, who was his designated successor, but had died at a very young age. The building could hold 15,000 spectators and for some events it could probably take as many as 20,000. Nevertheless, it was one of the smallest of its kind in Rome. The building was used as a theater until around AD 400 when its walls were plundered for stone for other buildings. In the 13th century, the Savellis,

Next to the Teatro di Marcello you can still see three Corinthian columns and part of a frieze (large picture and top right), which once belonged to the Temple of Apollo. Here the Romans stored many of the works of art that they had plundered from the Greeks in the 2nd century BC. The choice of a site close to the temple was deliberate – after all, Apollo was not only the god of prophecy but also the god of poetry.

one of the most noble families in the city, ordered its conversion into a fortress. Later, the two floors of arcades were shored up from the outside and apartments built on top; in the 16th century it was redeveloped again into a luxurious palace for the Orsinis, another aristocratic Italian family.

From the city's earliest days, there were many places where people could gather together in addition to the Forum Romanum. However, they were almost exclusively devoted to the sale of food and other goods, or domestic animals. The most important were the Forum Holitorium, the vegeta-ble market, and the Forum Boarium, the cattle market. Both were located close to the ancient port on the Tiber, where there was also a temple (later converted into a Christian church) devoted to the Portunus, the patron saint of ports. The area that once made up the cattle market is today

called the Piazza della Bocca della Verità – named after a stone mask of a Triton (god of the sea) dating from the 4th century BC, built into the portico of the church of Santa Maria in Cosmedin. The ancient stone is likely to have been a drainage channel cover – a sad use for the effigy of a god.

According to legend, if a liar places a hand in the Bocca della Verità (Mouth of Truth, above), it will bite off their fingers. Large picture: The church of Santa Maria in Cosmedin dates from the 6th century. Inside it is adorned with marble furnishings created by the Cosmati brothers from the 13th century.

In the 4th century, the historian Ammianus Marcellinus wrote about the members of the "people of base extraction": "These men spend their whole lives in drinking, and gambling, and brothels, and pleasures, and public spectacles; and to them the Circus Maximus is their temple, their home." When it was built some 800 years earlier, the complex did not have such a bad reputation. According to legend an arena for horse races had been built in the marshy valley between the Palatine and the Aventine hills during the reign of King Tarquinius Priscus (616-579 BC. At that time, spectators

still sat on very basic wooden seats, but Julius Caesar demanded that the arena be totally re-designed. Under the orders of Augustus an obelisk of Ramses II from Heliopolis was erected on the central line of the racetrack; in 1589 it was moved to the Piazza del Popolo by Pope Sixtus V.

An empty space exists on the area of the former complex on the Via del Circo Massimo (large picture). Only a few ruins of individual structures (above: the ruins of the former southern stand) recall the splendor and the glory of the past. The racetrack is formed by a 590-m-long (1,936-ft) oval that is divided in the middle by a 1.75-m-tall (5.75-ft) and 5.8-m-wide (19-ft) wall, the *spina*.

One of the first great pleasure palaces constructed for the people was the hippodrome, Circus Maximus dating from the 4th century BC. Light, two-wheeled chariots raced around the oval arena, pulled by two to seven horses. Fatal crashes were quite frequent, though it was far less gruesome entertainment than the games held in the large amphitheaters. Built between AD 72 and 80, the largest of these, the Coliseum, was particularly famous. It could seat around 50,000 spectators – or as many as 70,000 according to some estimates, making it the largest amphitheater in the Roman world. The seating was strictly regimented: the best seats, identified by name, were reserved for the emperor, the magistrate, and the vestal virgins. The senators had a row of seats made from ivory. Women were at the very top in the worst seats. A giant bright sail, the velarium, could be stret-

ched across the Coliseum to protect the head of the spectators from the blazing sun. Gladiators fought against each other and if the emperor gave the infamous "thumbs down" sign, the loser was killed by the victor. Thousands of gladiators – and animals – lost their lives. at the official opening.

Panem et circenses – bread and games – so wrote the Roman orator and poet Juvenal (c. 60 to128) in his *Satires*: That's all you need to satisfy a people, was the sober consideration of his contemporaries. *Circenses* in Latin could mean circus games but also chariot races – covering both of the two most common mass spectacles of the day; *panem* was available in the form of the donation of grains.

The Romans enjoyed a well-developed bathing culture. As early as the 2nd century BC public bathing facilities were widely available, and everyone could go there for a small fee. Inside, the baths featured a caldarium (a room with hot, moist air), a tepidarium (a warm room), a frigidarium (a cold room), various heat locks, covered walkways, a gymnasium for wrestling and boxing, a swimming pool, and other facilities. Heating was spread under the floor of the building, which was raised on pillars. The imperial baths developed out of the fact that the Roman emperors knew that they could

The marble bust of Caracalla, a gallant fresco, and a floor mosaic (above and large picture) attest to the highly developed bathing culture, at the Caracalle Baths, begun under Emperor Septimius Severus in 206 and inaugurated by Caracalla in 216. Around 1900, an archaeological park was set up on the grounds of the Caracalla Baths – a green space that extended from the Aurelian Wall to the heart of the city (top right).

buy the goodwill of the people by opening facilities such as baths, which were used for personal hygiene and leisure. One of the great bathing complexes was the Caracalla Baths (Terme di Caracalla), which could cater for 1,600 at a time, and up to 6,000 people visited the imperial complex daily.

If you arrive in Rome by train, you will discover enormous stone blocks on the square in front of the Stazione Termini: After Rome was invaded by the Gauls in 370 BC, the Servian Walls were erected, the first defensive walls to be built around Rome. They were 11.5 km (7 miles) long and had 16 gates. Construction of a new wall did not begin until the time of Emperor Aurelian (270–275) and was completed under his successor Probus. From the dimensions of the Aurelian Walls, it is evident just how much larger Rome had become since the city was attacked by the Gauls: the new

It is thanks to the Aurelian Walls (large picture) that Rome survived the period of the Migration Period relatively unscathed. Above: the Pyramid of Cestius stands in the middle of the city fortifications, on the road to Ostia. It is 27 m (89 ft) high, and its sides measure 22 m (72 ft). The pyramid stands on a travertine base, covered with slabs of white Carrara marble. An inscription reads that it was built in 330 days, and once had a gilded tip.

walls were 18 km (11 miles) long, 17 m (55 ft) high and 4 m (13 ft) wide, and had no less than 381 towers and parts are still standing today. The Pyramid of Cestius near the Porta San Paolo is the tomb of Caius Cestius Epulonius (d. 12 BC) and is a reminder of the enthusiasm for Egypt at that time.

The Via Appia, constructed in 312 BC, served as both a military and trading route. Extended many times over the centuries, it led across the Italian peninsula to Brindisi. In around 450 BC, it was forbidden to bury the dead in the city, so the inhabitants of Rome began to inter their loved ones beside the arterial roads, which is why the Via Appia is lined with numerous family and communal graves. Today, the official start of the Via Appia is no longer in the Roman Forum, but at the Porta San Sebastiano, the city gate in the Aurelian Walls. Approximately 3 km (2 miles) out from the city is an imposing circular stone build-

ing, approximately 20 m (65 ft) in diameter. It contains the tomb of Cecilia Metella, the wife of a patrician. Under the ground on either side of the Via Appia is the enormous network of labyrinth catacombs, the burial places of the early Christians, which were spread out beneath the fields.

The Via Appia Antica, fringed by cypresses and pine trees, has some sections on which the original cobble stones still lie – these convey a particularly haunting image of the days when Romans used to bury their dead under torch light at night.

A mass was celebrated in the Sistine Chapel on the 500th anniversary of the Swiss Guards: the men in their famous Renaissance uniforms have been protecting the pope and his residence since 1506.

THE VATICAN

The Via della Conciliazione, begun in 1937 and completed 13 years later, in 1950, connects St Peter's Square to the Castel Sant'Angelo on the western bank of the Tiber River. The road not only provides a physical link between Rome and the Vatican City, it is also a symbol of the reconciliation (conciliazione) between the Church and state that was achieved through the Lateran Pact of 1929. After Italy's unification in 1870, the popes had to relinquish their position as secular rulers; the Lateran Pact recognized the Vatican as an independent state, and the pope still bears the title "Sovereign of the State of the Vatican City".

The papacy has enjoyed a longer tradition than any other institution in the world. Uniting over one billion Catholics in their faith, it is global in the best sense of the word. Its ceremonies and rituals are carried out with pomp and magnificence, which sets them apart from everyday life. In his role as head of the Roman Catholic Church the pope is the focal point of the Catholic religion, therefore the reputation of the papacy and the Catholic Church is inextricably linked with the character of the man holding the office. The history of the papacy is marked by highs and lows and unfortunately not all popes in the past have been of pristine character. Some were notorious in their extravagance and lust for power, and some did not follow their own teaching, their real interest lying in the power of the highest office in the Catholic Church, rather than proclaiming the word of God.

Touching the foot of the bronze statue of St. Peter (above), probably created by Arnolfo di Cambio and standing in the main aisle of the St. Peter's Cathedral, is said to bring blessings. Boniface VIII (real name Benedetto Caetani, pope 1294–1303) introduced the Holy Year (anno santo) in 1300. The medieval illumination (large picture) shows him at the College of Cardinals. Top right: the popes John XXIII, John Paul II, and Benedict XVI.

As the original bishop of Rome, Peter was also the first to hold the title of pope. According to the words of Jesus taken from the Gospel and inscribed on the internal frieze of the great dome of St Peter's: "You are Peter, the Rock, and on this rock I will build my church" (Matthew 16,18).

The occupants of the Apostolic See did not always confine themselves to their roles as spiritual leaders of Christendom, but increasingly developed into political leaders. In 754 the – Catholic – king of the Franks, Pepin the Short gifted extensive territories on the Italian peninsula to the Church. These laid the foundation for the Papal States, which expanded over the centuries in the north to Tuscany and as far as Naples in the south. In 1075 Gregory VII announced that the spiritual as well as the political power of the pope exceeded that of any other Christian – including that of the emperor. During the papacy of Innocent III (1198–1216) the theocracy reached its climax. However, in 1309, Pope Clement V, a Frenchman, moved the popes' residence to Avignon and thus into the sphere of influence of the French monarchy. Although Gregory XI returned the papal see to Rome in 1377, the many

THE STORY OF THE PAPAL STATES

decades during which Rome was no longer the sole seat of the head of Christendom had brought dire consequences for the city. The number of inhabitants had decreased greatly and many important monuments and buildings, particularly religious one had been allowed to fall into disrepair.

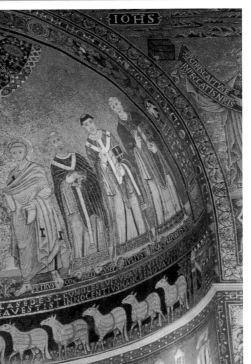

Santa Maria in Trastevere (large picture: the mosaics in the apse) is probably the oldest Church of St.Mary and the firstsite in Rome where the Christians were allowed to celebrate mass. Above: a fresco by Andrea Delitio depicting Gregory the Great in the Cathedral of S. Maria Assunta in Atri. Innocent III (real name Lotario dei Conti di Segni) is considered the most important pope in the Middle Ages (top: a fresco form 13th century).

The square is at its most beautiful when the sun has set, the tourists have gone, and the Roman night sky bathes the city in a magical light. Not actually square in shape, it was created at the height of the baroque period, after Luther's Protestant Reformation, when the Catholic Church wanted its sacred buildings to inspire awe in believers and reinforce its claim as the one true authority of God on earth. St Peter's Square is a beautiful forecourt to St Peter's Basilica. Designed by Bernini between 1656 and 1667, the square is 240 m (696 ft) wide, surrounded by colonnades of 284 columns topped by

140 statues of saints. To the left and right, at the two focal points of the giant oval, are two 14-m (46-ft) fountains. White marble stones are used as sundial markers, indicating the point where the tip of the obelisk's shadow lies at noon, as the sun enters each of the signs of the zodiac.

Monumental architecture: a view of St. Peter's through the colonnades. In the middle of the square is a 25-m-tall (82-foot) Egyptian obelisk, brought to Rome from Heliopolis by Emperor Caligula in AD 37 (large picture). Above: the dome of St. Peter's Basilica, designed by Michelangelo, is a prominent feature of Rome's skyline. Top: The faithful from all over the world come to this square.

Rome 107

Born on 5 December 1443 into a poor family in Albisola Superiore near Savona and raised by Franciscan monks, Giuliano della Rovere was chosen as the representative of Jesus Christ in earth on 1 November 1503 and from then on called himself Pope Julius II. Three years later he laid the foundation stone for the new St. Peter's Basilica. Critics claimed that he had only commissioned the giant church as an appropriate setting for the elaborate tomb designed for him by Michelangelo. Others thought the architect Bramante was the main manipulator responsible for the fact that the basilica that had stood on the likely tomb of the Apostle St. Peter since the 4th century was being demolished. Neither Bramante nor the pope, who entered the annals of history not only as a patron of the arts but also as a successful military commander, lived to see the new buidling completed. The pope recon-

quered territories that had been lost to the Papal States and founded a power like no other pope had ever possessed. However, his tomb was much smaller than originally planned by Michelangelo, and when Julius II died in 1513 it was placed not in St. Peter's but in San Pietro in Vincoli.

"There is no art in piling millions of tiles one on top of the other, but let Bramante create just one of those columns that he wants to destroy so reck lessly", said Michelangelo, whose vault spans the papal altar and Bernini's bronze canopy (large picture). Above: detail of the lying statue created by Maso del Bosco for the tomb of Julius' II. Top: Michelangelo and Pope Julius II in a painting by Anastasio Fontebuoni.

No other architect implemented the idea of the re-birth – the Renaissance – of Antiquity as systematically as Donato Bramante (c. 1444–1514). He became the master of the Greek cross or central-plan buildings where everything converged on one central vertical axis, as opposed to the Latin Cross or longitudinal plan as in, for example, the basilica. The architectural ideal of the central-plan building was effective beyond the Renaissance into the era of the Baroque. Bramante, who was a well respected master-builder thanks to his work in Milan and Pavia, came to Rome in 1499, and in 1503 he entered service for the new pope. During the reign of Julius II, Rome regained its position as capital of the arts. He took on the building of the new St. Peter's Basilica and entrusted Bramante with it. His design of a monumental centrallly planned building laid out as a giant square was, however, not exe-

The last years of Bramante's life were dominated by the rebuilding of St. Peter's Basilica (top right: copper engraving of St. Peter's Square, c. 1820). Bramante planned the church as a central-plan building in the shape of the Greek cross (large picture). After his death St. Peter's Basilica was built to the plans of Michelangelo, as a domed longitudinal building. Above: Bramante on a fresco fragment (Casa Grattaroli, Bergamo).

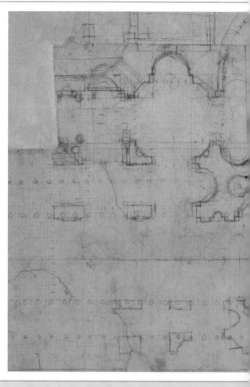

cuted as planned. It was decided after Bramante's death to return to the customary shapes of the longitudinal structure. Thus, the ancient round temple in the cloisters of San Pietro in Montorio at Rome remained the most important work of this master-builder.

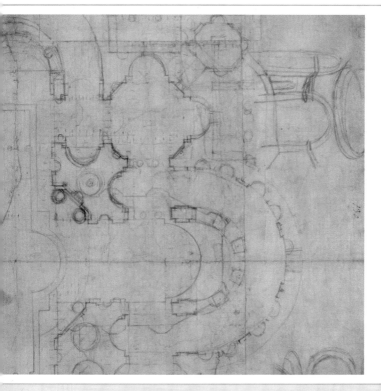

THE VATICAN

The present basilica, which was built from 1506 on the site of a former basilica commissioned by Emperor Constantine, was once the largest Christian church in the world, covering 15,000 sq m (161,400 sq ft). The façade is some 45 m (147 ft) high and 115 m (377 ft) wide, and the height to the lantern crowning the dome is 132 m (433 ft). The interior of the cathedral can hold 60,000 worshippers. Some of the most famous artists of their time worked on the design; architects Bramante and Sangallo, painters, Raphael and Michelangelo and sculptors, Bernini and Maderno. Near Bernini's

Building the new St. Peter's Basilica took around one and a half centuries in total. Despite the many architects who participated it is seamless, both inside and out (large picture and top right). Above the Cathedra Petri with the apse is an oval alabaster window depicting a dove, the symbol of the Holy Spirit (above) created by Bernini.

tomb of Urban VIII (real name Maffeo Barberini, pope 1623–1644) you can descend to the grottoes, where the tomb of Peter, is said to lie. There are some 100 tombs in St Peter's, including over 90 popes, and James Stuart, the "Old Pretender", son of the deposed James II of England.

To counter the aesthetic imbalance that he feared would develop when the original plan for creating St. Peter as a centrally planned structure was changed into a longitudinal building, Bernini designed a baldachin, a canopy-like structure, for the papal altar. With help from his assistant Francesco Borromini, he designed the dome of the St. Peter's Basilica as an optical reconciliation between the two different directions: a giant stage set in which his baldachin marked the real heart of the church interior as well as drawing attention from all directions. The baldachin is

supported by four spiralled columns, and bears a gilded cross on top of a sphere symbolizing the world. The underside of the baldachin has a radiant sun. It stands on marble bases decrated with the three bees, heraldic emblems of the Barberini family of Pope Urban VIII.

In the dome space of St. Peter's Basilica, right above the supposed tomb of St. Peter, stands the papal altar, crowned by a 29-m-tall (95-ft) bronze baldachin created by Bernini on the orders of Pope Urban VIII between 1624 and 1633. The canopy was made from the melted down bronze decorations from the roof of the Pantheon so that at the time the Romans mocked: "What the barbarians didn't do, the Barberini did."

The present St. Peter's Basilica extends across three levels from different periods of architectural history: the new building; the level of the Vatican or Sacred Grottoes underneath it, resting on Constantine's old St. Peter's Basilica; and the even lower level of the Vatican necropolis, which was only excavated under Pope Pius XII in the 20th century during the search for the historical tomb of St. Peter. The center of the Vatican Grottoes is formed by a circular crypt linked to a three-aisled hall space. The "new" grottoes are reached via a corridor (in fact, these are older, but they were restored

more recently). The "old" grottoes is situated off a three-aisled hall where the tombs of many cardinals and popes can be visited, including that of John Paul II. Below the hall, is the Vatican necropolis with two open tombs and 18 mausoleums on an ancient road of tombs.

A narrow staircase inside the front right pillar in the crossing leads down to the grottoes (top). Aside from John Paul II (large picture: Pope Benedict XVI at the tomb of his predecessor) many popes found their final resting place here, both from the Old St. Peter's Basilica as well as many of Christ's representatives who have died since but for whom there was no space in the new St. Peter's Basilica.

Along with Italian master, Leonardo da Vinci, Michelangelo Buonarroti (1475–1564) is the most important artist of the country's high Renaissance. The creative focus for this brilliant painter, sculptor, and architect was the human figure. Michelangelo learned fresco painting as a pupil of Domenico Ghirlandaio and looked to the old masters for inspiration, studying the sculptures of the ancient world. In order to achieve perfection in his representation of human anatomy, he is said not only to have drawn from life, but also to have secretly dissected corpses. In 1505 Pope Julius II summoned the artist to Rome to design a prestigious papal tomb, but when both this commission and his plans for a new St Peter's Basilica were rejected, Michelangelo returned, disenchanted, to Florence. However, a new challenge was to draw him back to Rome: the painting of the ceiling of the Sistine Chapel. Michelangelo

Above: a portrait of the artist, known as Michelagniolo di Lodovico di Leonardo di Buonarroto Simoni, by one of his pupils, painted around 1510. Among the main pieces Michelangelo created as a sculptor were Pietà in St. Peter's Basilica (large picture) and his David in Florence. Equally famous is the statue of Moses, created between 1513 and 1516, in the church of San Pietro in Vincoli (top right).

spent four years on this project, working virtually alone. High above ground balancing on scaffolding, the work was also physically exremely demanding. In 1547, he took over the supervision of the rebuilding of St Peter's: its dome being undoubtedly his greatest architectural achievement.

The Sistine Chapel was commissioned by Pope Sixtus IV in 1477, after whom it is named. Not only a place of devotion, it was also a fortress, with walls 3 m (nearly 10 ft) thick, and still serves today as the place where the cardinals hold papal conclaves, the ceremony in which a new pope is elected. Sixtus had been at war with Florence, but by the time the chapel was completed, in 1480, the war was over and as a gesture of peace Lorenzo de' Medici, the ruler of Florence, sent some of his city's leading painters to Rome to decorate the interior of the chapel. The artists included Perugino, Bot-

...ticelli, and Ghirlandaio. The walls of the Chapel were painted with scenes from the lives of Jesus and Moses, and the barrel-vaulted ceiling was transformed into a radiant blue sky with golden stars. Some 20 years later, Pope Julius II commissioned Michelangelo to repaint the ceiling.

The side walls of the Sistine Chapel show scenes from the lives of Christ and Moses. Michelangelo's altar fresco illustrates the Last Judgment (large picture); he also created the ceiling fresco (top: The Creation of Adam, above: The Fall of Man and the Expulsion from the Garden of Eden and The Separation of Land and Water) featuring topics from the creation and the fall of man.

THE VATICAN

Many popes were avid collectors, while others commissioned works of art in the role of both patron and client. Today, the complex of Vatican Museums – located in a major part of the Vatican palaces along the Viale Vaticano – holds one of the largest collections of art in the world, with exhibits ranging from ancient Egyptian and Etruscan objects to modern sacred art. The Pinacoteca (art gallery), opened by Pius XI in 1932, displays paintings from the 11th to the 19th centuries. The Missionary-Ethnological Museum brings objects together from wherever the Catholic Church has been

Allow sufficient time to visit the Vatican Museums (above: the staircase spiraling its way upward; large picture: a gallery of sculptures) so you can do justice to their exceptional wealth in art treasures from the exceptionally ancient Orient and Antiquity up to the present day. Top right: Raphael's ceiling frescoes in the Stanza della Segnatura, which was once used as a study.

active in its mission work around the world. In 2000, John Paul II officially opened the new entrance to the complex, featuring a huge spiral ramp reminiscent of New York's Guggenheim Museum. In his inaugural speech, John Paul II called the Vatican Museums "a bridge to the world".

Three geniuses left their mark on the Italian high Renaissance: Leonardo da Vinci, Michelangelo, and Raphael. Born in Urbino in 1483, Raphael's fame outshone that of any other painter for centuries, and no other artist was so widely imitated. The two quizzical and charming putti that Raphael added to his Sistine Madonna have been reproduced on millions of gift cards and souvenirs (the original is located in the Gemäldegalerie, Dresden, Germany). Raphael's work was famous for its perfection and grace – the men and women in Raphael's paintings seem almost too beautiful to be true. He was accused by many of superficiality, which may be true for some of his religious paintings, but Raphael worked with the intensity and individuality of a true master, especially in regard to his portraits. He moved to Rome in 1508, when, at the height of his creativity and inundated with orders, Pope Julius II com-

missioned him to paint frescoes in a suite of rooms now known as the stanze. In 1514, he took over the management of the rebuilding of St Peter's Basilica, and in 1515 he was also given the responsibility of excavating and recording Roman antiquities. He was just 37 when he died of a fever in 1520.

For the Vatican Raphael created the paintings *The Fire in the Borgo* (1514, top) and *The School of Athens* (1510–1511, large picture), among others. The former shows Leo IV (pope 847–855) blessing the people from the benediction loggia, which miraculously extinguishes the fire and saves church and people. Raphael painted his self-portrait (above) in 1506.

If you calculate the value of the works kept stored there, the Vatican Library is the richest library in the world. The catalog produced by the first prefect, Bartolomeo Sacchi, listed 3,400 volumes in 1481, and the Codex Vaticanus, the oldest known manuscript of the Greek Bible, came into the library's possession in 1448. From 2007 to 2010 these bibliophile treasures remained concealed from the public because of restoration work. Now the Salone Sistino, or Sistine Hall, the historic heart of the papal book collection, which for years could only be reached on guided tours of the

Vatican Museums, has now reopened to the public. It was incorporated into the library as a reading room with chained-down books. The Salone Sistino was originally built between 1587 and 1590 on the orders of Pope Sixtus V; it is the work of the Renaissance architect Domenico Fontana.

A fresco by Melozzo da Forlì (1438–1494) of Pope Sixtus IV, after whom the Salone Sistino is named. He is shown naming Bartolomeo Platina as the director of the Vatican Library (top). The library comprises a long network of corridors (large picture) and rooms (above: a ceiling fresco). Particularly valuable collection pieces are exhibited in glass cabinets, among them the records of Galilei and other manuscripts.

At nightfall on 22 January 1506, a group of 150 Swiss men from the canton of Uri, commanded by Captain Kaspar von Silnen, marched via the Porta del Popolo into the Vatican, where they were blessed by Pope Julius II. That day is considered the official birth of the Swiss Guards, formed for the personal protection of the pope – although in 1479, Sixtus IV had made an alliance with the Confederates, which allowed for the recruitment of mercenaries. The driving force behind the intervention by the Swiss on behalf of Julius II was Matthäus Schiner, the bishop of Sitten in the Valais canton. Borninto a family of farmers in Mühlbach, he was initially educated by his uncle who was the vicar of the village. He continued his studies at Zürich, Como, and in Rome where he was consecrated as a priest in 1489. Once he had become a bishop he championed the alliance between Pope Julius II

The Swiss Guards were called the "Defenders of the Church's freedom" by Pope Julius II. They look back on a tradition of more than 500 years as the personal bodyguards of the Pope. Large picture: newly sworn in guards take part in a mass in St. Peter's Basilica; top right: a look behind the scenes.

and the Helvetians. Today the Swiss Guard is the last remainder of the once powerful army of the Papal States, and they still swear in their oath today, "to … serve the reigning Pope [name of Pope] and his legitimate successors, and … should it become necessary, even my own life …".

Emperor Hadrian (76–138) built the Castel Sant'Angelo as a mausoleum, but from the 9th century it was gradually converted into a papal fortress by successive popes. In the 14th century, a secret underground passage, the Passetto di Borgo, was constructed to connect the fortress with the papal palace. It was put to good use during the Sack of Rome in 1527, when Pope Clement VII and his cardinals escaped from the soldiers of Holy Roman Emperor Charles V. Among the defenders was goldsmith and sculptor Benvenuto Cellini, who was so accurate as a gunner and killed so many of the opposing

The Way of the Cross: In 1667 Pope Clement IX commissioned Bernini, the master-builder of the Baroque, to create eight white marble statues for the Ponte Sant'Angelo – in the event there were ten. Bernini's pupils carried out his designs for the Passion of Christ; each angels carries an instrument of Christ's suffering.

troops that he later suffered pangs of remorse. However, as Cellini wrote in his autobiography, the pope "raised his hand and made the sign of the cross over my whole body, blessed me and forgave me all my murderous deeds that I had ever committed in the service of the Apostolic Church".

As well as St. Peter's, Rome has three other patriarchal basilicas, defined as churches that have a papal throne and an altar at which only the pope may read the mass: San Paolo fuori le Mura, Santa Maria Maggiore, and San Giovanni in Laterano. As its name indicates ("basilica outside the walls") San Paolo fuori le Mura lies to the south, beyond the city walls. The vast basilica, founded in the 4th century, was almost completely destroyed by fire in July 1823, but was reconstructed using materials from several countries, including Egypt (alabaster pillars) and Russia (lapis lazuli and

The stunning coffered ceiling was splendidly reconstructed (above) as were the mosaics on the façade (large picture). The mosaics in the apse (top right) show Christ with Peter, Andrew, Luke, and Paul.

malachite). The main door incorporates part of the original door. The mosaics have also been renewed. The 13th-century cloisters, with highly decorated and shaped columns, survived the fire. The church is dedicated to St. Paul, who died a martyr's death in Rome, and is said to be buried here.

Legend has it that in 352 the Virgin Mary appeared to Pope Liberius in a dream, and commanded him to build a church in the place where he'd see snow fall the next morning. As snow is a very rare sight in Rome at any time of year, it is quite miraculous when it does occur – as in this case – on 5 August. When he awoke and saw the peak of the Esquiline Hill covered in a layer of white, Liberius lost no time in obeying the will of the Virgin. To commemorate the miracle responsible for the construction of the basilica, a service takes place every August in which white petals are scattered down on

The three-aisled interior of Santa Maria Maggiore (large picture; above: a detail) still recalls the original edifice. In the Middle Ages a bell tower was added, while the waffle-slab ceiling dates from the Renaissance. Top right: one of the two domes; like the façade these dates from the baroque period.

the worshippers. Despite being damaged in the earthquake of 1348, the church retains the core of its original structure from the 5th century AD. The structure of the church was repeatedly changed over the centuries and today is a temple of different styles in art and architecture. through the ages.

The district in which this basilica lies is named after the once powerful Laterani family, who were disgraced at the start of the 4th century. Their land was confiscated by Emperor Constantine and used to build the first Christian basilica. It burned down twice, and was reconstructed in its original form on each occasion. Architect Borromini altered parts of the interior in 1646 and in the 18th century a new huge façade was added. For Catholics, the Lateran basilica is the "mother of all churches", ranking even higher than St. Peter's Basilica. The church lies on the southern side of the

Palazzo Lateranense, the papal residence until the start of the 13th century. The Scala Santa (Holy Staircase), opposite the palace, is a place of pilgrimage for many – the feet of Jesus allegedly touched the steps as he was led to Pontius Pilate. Pilgrims must climb it on their hands and knees.

The Battistero San Giovanni in Fonte, the baptistery of San Giovanni in Laterano (large picture and above) was built in the 4th century, during the reign of Constantine. It stands on a octagonal ground plan – the number 8 symbolizes the "Eighth Day of Creation", the resurrection of Christ, and the re-creation of humanity by God. Top: the Holy Staircase that is said to have once stood in the palace of Pontius Pilate.

At night "across the Tibers": The view over the rooftops of the Eternal City shows the different worlds which inhabit this magnificent capital. It could almost be a set for a Fellini movie.

BEYOND ROME

In many ways, Rome is a city of contrasts. Aside from the clash of Old and New, you are also immersed into entirely different world from one part of town to another. In the working-class district of Testaccio there is a lively hustle and bustle, whereas on the tranquil Aventine Hill you could almost forget that you are in the middle of a great city. On the margins of the city you'll find the Renaissance and baroque villas of the nobility and of high-ranking clerics' in the "borgate". Meanwhile, 1960s tenement blocks, once documented by the film maker, Pier Paolo Pasolini dominate the Roman suburbs.

One year after Julius III (real name Giovanni Maria Ciocchi del Monte, pope 1550–1555) had been chosen as the supreme head of the Catholic church, he commissioned the architects Vasari, Vignola, and Ammanati to build a suburban summer residence for him. A magnificent complex, surrounded by sumptuous gardens, was created between 1551 and 1553, which combined architecture, nature, water features, and art in a glorious setting. Since 1989 the Mannerist-style villa has been home to the Museo Nazionale Etrusco, the National Etruscan Museum. Visitors reach the

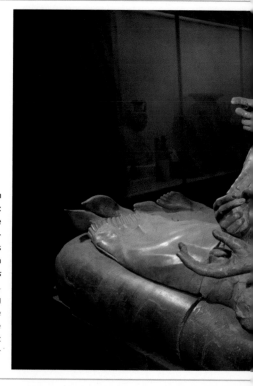

With the end of papal power in 1870 the Villa Giulia (top right: the front of the villa, facing the Via Flaminia) fell to the kingdom of Italy. The most famous exhibit in the Etruscan Museum is the *Sarcophagus of the Spouses* (c. 510 BC) from Cerveteri, depicting the couple half lying and half seated as if they were at an ancient banquet. The woman's gesture suggests that she is pouring perfume into her husband's hand (large picture).

Nymphaeum via a columned hall. Like a multi-level theater, the villa's niches were adorned with statues – attesting to the pope's love of all things ancient. The fountain in the centre, the Fontanadell' Acqua Vergine, is fed by the same source as the Fontana di Trevi in Rome's Centro Storico.

The Villa Borghese was built on the northern limit of the city, between 1613 and 1616, not far from the Villa Giulia and surrounded by the vineyards of the Borghese family. It was once owned by Cardinal Scipione Caffarelli Borghese, an important patron of the arts and a nephew of Paul V's (real Camillo Borghese, pope 1605–1621). The villa also comprised a splendid park, which was transformed as an English garden at the end of the 18th century and then became a public park featuring fountains, pavilions, and follies of ruins. Today it is joined with the Pinicio, making it one of the most

beautiful parks in Rome. Since 1911 a small zoo, the Giardino Zoologico has been housed here. The Casino Borghese, built by the Dutchman Jan van Santen between 1613 and 1615, was converted to a museum, and now holds the impressive Borghese collection of antiques and paintings.

Among other works, the Museo e Galleria Borghese (top: view of the outside; above Mariano Rossi's baroque ceiling frescoes in the hall in the entrance area) exhibits numerous statues created by Bernini for Cardinal Scipione Caffarelli Borghese. Particularly famous is Bernini's sculpture *The Rape of Proserpina* dating from 1621 (large picture, in the foreground), which looks magnificent from whichever side it is viewed.

The district of San Lorenzo, just outside Rome's eastern walls, suffered serious bomb damage during World War II. The basilica of the same name – dedicated to St. Laurence, who died a martyr's death for his faith in 258 – was also damaged, but has been restored. It was founded during the reign of the emperor Constantine (4th century), but has been altered and extended many times since then. Today's San Lorenzo fuori le Mura was formed when the existing St Laurence's church was joined with an adjacent church dedicated to the Virgin Mary. The relics of St. Laurence and other saints are stored

After St Laurence was tortured to death on a burning hot rack and buried here, his tomb became a place of pilgrimage (large picture: the chancel of the San Lorenzo fuori le Mura Basilica). The adjoining Campo Verano is the largest cemetery in the metropolis on the Tiber, well worth a visit for its elaborate tombs, mausoleums, and monuments (top right: mourning turned to stone).

here; San Lorenzo also houses the sarcophagus of Pius IX (real name Giovanni Maria Mastai-Ferretti, pope 1846–1878); often regarded as the first modern pope, he was the last ruler of the independent Papal States, before the papacy was reduced to just a spiritual, rather than a political force.

The Tiber, cloudy and grey, flows erratically and "often causes great damage". This was the harsh verdict of Swiss scholar Johann Jacob Grasser in an early travel guide dating from 1609. In order to control its flow – or overflow, as it flooded regularly – high embankments were constructed in the 1870s, forcing the river to stay in its bed. Despite having had its excesses tamed, the Tiber has still not lost any of its magic, and a walk along its banks is a treat on a warm evening – perhaps to the Ponte Fabricio, one of the oldest bridges in the city. This leads to the Isola Tiberina, an island

lying in the river like a ship at anchor opposite what used to be the old port of Ostia. After an epidemic in 291 BC, a temple was erected on the island, dedicated to Aesculapius, the god of healing. The church of San Bartolomeo was built on the ruins of this pagan place of worship in the 10th century.

Rome was founded (large picture) where Il Tevere, the Tiber, flows around a bend. Above: a fountain sculpture of the Tiber on the Piazza del Campidoglio. Top: hardy Romans traditionally greet the New Year by jumping into the river for a refreshing swim.

For many a Roman born on the right bank of the Tiber, visiting the Trastevere quarter – which literally translates as "across the Tiber" – is almost like going abroad. But naturally, the inhabitants of this area, which was settled at a later date (around 500 BC, although in Rome the term is relative), are proud to live here: they don't think of themselves as Romans but rather as "Trasteverini". The layout of the streets also demonstrates that they have maintained a certain independence from the rest of the city; visitors to the area can only find their way around the picturesque labyrinth of narrow alleyways by following the high bell towers of the Romanesque churches. Despite the washing lines often strung high up across the streets between buildings, the cliché of a poor but tightly knit Italian city community is not entirely accurate: in the 1970s the Travestere area became fashionable,

and therefore more expensive. Many of the artisans, students, and artists were driven out often after battles with developers. But not all of the small traditional stores have given way to chic bars and boutiques. You can still find the original Trastevere today, hidden away in the maze of alleyways.

Lively and full of joie de vivre – people in the "other" Rome also enjoy dining in one of the many street cafés (large picture). They also admire the patience and precision with which the watchmakers on the Vicolo del Cedro do their work (top); and they also enjoy the wide variety of bric-a-brac available on the Sunday flea market at the Porta Portese (above).

The Piazza di Santa Maria in Trastevere is regarded as the heart of this district. The octagonal fountain in the middle of the square, redesigned by Carlo Fontana in 1692, was originally one of the oldest in Rome. Santa Maria in Trastevere is probably the oldest church of St. Mary in the city, founded on the spot where – according to legend – a source of oil was said to have sprung from the ground in 38 BC; it was interpreted by the Jews as a sign announcing the coming of the Messiah and later by the Christians as proof that the redeemer was approaching. Inside the church an inscription

behind the right-hand chancel points out the "fons olei", the spot where the spring was said to have been. The church is on the site of an earlier structure from the 3rd and 4th centuries during the reign of Trastevere-born, Innocent II (real name Gregorio Papareschi di Guidoni, pope 1130–1143).

From the fountain in the middle of the square you get the best view of Santa Maria in Trastevere. The church's mosaic frieze (12th–14th centuries), which displays Byzantine influences, depicts Mary and the child among ten female saints (large picture and top). The most significant art treasure inside the three-aisled Church of St. Mary are the superb mosaics in the apse, created during the 12th and 13th centuries (above).

Cecilia, born into a noble Roman family around 200, was raised as a Christian right from her birth. Her parents forced her to marry a pagan young man, Valerianus, but Cecilia managed to convert her husband and his brother to Christianity. The both died a martyr's death, and only a short time later Cecilia was sentenced to be executed: according to legend, the Prefect Almachius ordered her to be placed in a boiling hot bath, but this caused her no harm. The executioner then tried to behead her three times with his sword – yet Cecilia lived for a further three days and bequeathed all

her earthly goods to the poor. She was finally buried in the Calixtus Catacombs. It was believed a church was built in the 4th or 5th century, on the remains of the house where Cecilia and Valerianus lived; it was enlarged and redesigned several times. Her skull is kept in the cathedral of Torcello.

The choir of the church of Santa Cecilia in Trastevere boasts an impressive ciborium (large picture) created by Arnolfo di Cambio in 1283. Also in the 13th century, Pietro Cavallini painted his fresco, *Last Judgment* (above: a detail). A carved marble image created by Stefano Maderno, circa 1600 lies under the altar (top); showing the saint in the body position in which she was found when her sarcophagus was opened in 1599.

Early Christians took special care of their dead. The community maintained its own cemeteries, and as early as the 3rd century it is possible to find the first documents attesting to modest artistic activities such as wall frescoes or the design of sarcophagi. The Christian community concerned themselves with the interment of their deceased and gave them a memorial beyond the death that would also intercede on their behalf – an expression of the exclusive self-image of these early Christians as a "community of saints", as "holy church", and as a "place of the supernatural" where God and man could be close to each other, even "encounter" each other. The term "catacomb" for the Roman necropolises of this Christian community, however, was only applied very much later – it is a derivation of the medieval landscape name ad catacumbas (meaning, near the hollow) for the

The Calixtus catacombs (large picture) are one of the largest burial complexes, dug into the underground in the first four centuries in Rome. Their wall frescoes reflect both philosophical and religious subjects of the time. In the Ipogeo di Via Dino Compagni (above) an "anatomy lesson" was found, and in the Priscilla catacombs a fresco reminiscent of a Christian portrayal of Mary (top right).

underground burial places of the San Sebastiano along the Via Appia. The term is also used to set it apart from the pagan hypogeum. Just as the latter serve a mystery cult, so the catacombs did not just serve for the burial of the dead alone, but also for the veneration of Christian martyrs.

Named after the Roman god Janus, Gianicolo (the Janiculum Hill) lies on the west bank of the Tiber. The Aurelian Wall was extended up the hill to keep the watermills on the Gianicolo, that were used to grind corn, within the confines of the city. Despite not being one of the classic Seven Hills of Rome, it has seen its share of significant historical events. In 1849, the national hero Giuseppe Garibaldi barricaded himself here against French troops, who crushed the short-lived Roman republic. Memorials to these conflicts, which were precursors to the unification of Italy, show Garibaldi on

The Fontana dell'Acqua Paola (top right), built on the Via Garibaldi between 1608 and 1613, makes for a perfect wedding photograph backdrop. From here, the Passeggiata del Gianicolo (large picture: with marble busts of Italian patriots) leads via the Gianicolo Hill to the Piazza della Rovere, located not far from the Vatican on the Tiber. On the hill, Garibaldi still rides his horse for the liberation of the people (above).

horseback, looking toward the Vatican and his wife Anita, also on horseback, a baby in one hand and a gun in the other. These figures are in marked contrast to the idyllic, leafy surroundings. The hill is much loved and offers superb views. A canon is fired at noon each day to mark the exact time.

Agostino Chigi (1465–1520), who commissioned the villa which was completed in 1511, was one of the most important bankers of his time. He chose an idyllic place for his refuge from the city, which was even then filled with hectic hustle and bustle. In 1508 he brought the architect and painter Baldassare Peruzzi from his hometown of Siena to Rome to design the building. Peruzzi created a villa which featured a fascinatingly modest exterior that was amazingly sumptuously furnished inside. Chigi was also a great sponsor of the arts and he commissioned some of the most famous pain-

ters of his day to work on the villa. A special friendship linked him with Raphael who came from Urbino. By all accounts they both lived life to the full, and the villa was the venue for many a glittering party. Cardinal Alessandro Farnese bought the villa in 1580, and today it is named after him.

Peruzzi created a cycle of works for the Loggia of Galatea depicting the constellation of the stars at the time the owner, Chigi, was born (top: *The Nymph Callisto on Jupiter's Chariot*, 1511). He painted stunning illusionist trompe-l'oeils in the Perspectives' Hall (1516). Above: one of Chigi's lovers was probably the model for the Grace on the left in Raphael's fresco *Cupid shows Psyche to the Graces* (1518) in the Loggia of Psyche.

The Aventine is the southernmost of the seven hills of Rome: its western slope runs down to the Tiber, from where there's a wonderful view of the Isola Tiberina and the Vatican on the other side of the river. At the top of the hill, crowned by the 5th-century basilica of Santa Sabina, the hectic life of the city seems far away, which is why it is one of the most popular residential areas in Rome. The Aventine Hill was initially occupied by merchants, who carried out their business on the quays along the Tiber; then the area became chic and the rich and famous built villas here. Empe-

ror Hadrian lived on the Aventine before he became ruler of the Roman Empire. The Protestant cemetery is between the Aventine and Testaccio and is where many foreigners who died in Rome are buried, including English poets John Keats, and Percy Bysshe Shelley who drowned off Livorno.

According to legend, the basilica of Santa Sabina (above) was founded in ad 425 on the site of a house belonging to Sabina, a rich Roman woman who converted to Christianity. Large picture: the pines make the Aventine Hill a green oasis.

Monte Testaccio, the "eighth hill of Rome", around 35 m (114 ft) high and located in the working-class area of the same name, is actually an artificial mound almost entirely composed of the broken remains of amphorae (*testae* in Latin) accumulated over the centuries. Amphorae were large clay pots used to store and transport food and wine from the nearby Tiber port, which disappeared long ago. In the 19th century, the hill was a place of pilgrimage, and its summit is still crowned by a cross. Monte Testaccio is now barred to visitors, as amateur archeologists couldn't resist taking home a

On the food markets of this working-class district, such as the one at the Porta Portese, the fish is always fresh and the traders have well-honed sales pitches (large picture and above). At night people visit restaurants and bars (top right: the Via di Monte Testaccio).

fragment or two from the site. In the 19th century, Testaccio was a residential area for workers at the slaughterhouse and gas works. Since then, the area has become trendy with restaurants, bars, and cultural events. Former slaughterhouse, Ex Mattatoio, at the foot of the hill, is now a popular venue.

BEYOND ROME

As an exercise to display the glory of fascism, the EUR never quite came to fruition. Mussolini planned a World Exhibition for 1942, set in the southern part of Rome, with residential areas, museums, and parks. World War II intervened, and although the Esposizione Universale di Roma (EUR), the Universal Rome Exhibition, never materialized, by 1938, construction was already well underway. Inevitably, as with many projects pursued by Mussolini, the existing buildings made way for the new. The most notable building in the EUR – today a popular residential and business area – is

Mussolini's urbis magna, a fascist megalopolis, was intended to recall the imperial Rome of Antiquity. Its most distinctive structure is the Palazzo della Civiltà del Lavoro, the "Square Coliseum" (large picture). The statues symbolize the arts and various professions (above and top right).

Palazzo della Civiltà del Lavoro, nicknamed "the Square Coliseum". It is proof of Mussolini's and the fascists' desire to link their rule with that of the Roman Empire of Antiquity. The complex contains the Museum of Roman Civilization – a municipal history collection dedicated to ancient Rome.

Some 20 km (12 miles) south of the city, lies the famous Cinecittà film studio complex, built on the orders of Mussolini in 1937. It covers approximately 600,000 sq m (717,600 sq yds). Vast water tanks enable film production companies to re-create sea battles – just as the ancient Romans did when they flooded the Coliseum and the Piazza Navona, creating artificial lakes for the same purpose. In 1997, Cinecittà was privatized by the Italian government. The 1950s saw the production of the epic *Ben Hur* with its famous chariot race, while more recently Martin Scorsese's *The Gangs of New York* was shot here. The studios are also used by international TV companies such as the BBC and HBO. Legendary films shot in the studios include Federico Fellini's *La Dolce Vita* (1960), starring Marcello Mastroianni and Anita Ekberg, about the dark side of Roman high society in the 1960s and

CINECITTÀ – THE ROMAN DREAM FACTORY

the meaning of life – and love. In Fellini's *Roma* (1972), the city itself is the subject of the film, with Anna Magnani – a Roman unlike Fellini himself who came from Rimini, playing her last role. For many she was the representation of a *Romana*, hot-blooded and proud, and warm-hearted and lovable.

Passion turned legend: Marcello Mastroianni and Anita Ekberg in *La Dolce Vita* (large picture and above). It was the first film Mastroianni shot with Fellini, after which he became the director's acting alter ego. Top from the left: the film stars Anna Magnani and Sophia Loren and director and actor Roberto Benigni.

There are quiet places in Rome where you can escape the bustle and relax but these are not easy to find. Sometimes you just have to get out of the city – to Tivoli, for example and the fountains of the Villa d'Este.

THE ROMAN COUNTRYSIDE AND THE SEA

Even in ancient times, the Romans felt the need, particularly in the scorching hot summer, to escape from the hectic life in the big city on the Tiber. Those who could afford it bought a villa in the country, where they could relax and recoup their energies in a tranquil green space – Cicero's estate at Tusculum was particularly famous. These days, there is still an exodus from the city on public holidays and during the hot, summer months: the inhabitants of the capital are extremely privileged in that they have the sea on their doorstep to one side and the open countryside, the *campagna*, and the mountains on the other.

Only very few great cultures shone as brightly and were extinguished as quickly as that of the Etruscans. The Etruscan people, whose origins are unknown, spread out from their relatively small ancestral home land between the rivers Arno and Tiber on the Tyrrhenian side of the Italian peninsula. Roman historian Livius reported that, at the height of its dominance "so great was the power of Etruria that the renown of her people had filled not only the inland parts of Italy but also the coastal districts along the whole length of the land from the Alps to the Straits of Messina". The Etruscans formed city-states, which were ruled by kings until the end of the 6th century BC. From the 5th century BC they were ruled by senior magistrates and united in the Etruscan League of twelve states. The Etrucans fate was sealed, however, with the rise of Rome, and this culture vanished in the

mists of history. The Etruscans had a fatalist view of the role of divine powers in the shaping of human fates. At the same time their culture overflowed with the joy of living. They created one of the most progressive civilizations and bequeathed penmanship and the alphabet to the Romans.

Significant sites where Etruscan cultural objects were found are Cerveteri and Tarquinia, Volterra, Arezzo, Perugia, Cortona, Chiusi, Populonia, Rusellae, Vulci, Veji, and Volsinii (Orvieto). Trough their trade relations with the Greeks, the Etruscans also acquired Corinthian ceramics and black-figure vase pottery, which influenced their own production. All the objects shown on these two pages were found at Cerveteri.

THE ROMAN COUNTRYSIDE AND THE SEA

Situated in the modern provinces of Rome and Viterbo, the towns of Cerveteri and Tarquinia are famous for their superb Etruscan necropolises. The tombs, which show the different burial practices of the earliest civilizations of the northern Mediterranean region, depict the everyday lives of the people who lived here. Cerveteri – known as Caere in ancient Rome – is famous for the variety of architectural styles of its sculptures and tombs; however, what they have in common is the desire of their designers to furnish them like dwellings. The tombs also tell of Etruscan home life

Greek influences are evident in the wall frescoes in the Etruscan tombs: The frescoes in the "Tomb of the Augurs" (above and top right, c. 530 BC) as well as the "Tomb of the Leopards", so called after the big cats that are depicted in the gable (large picture, c. 480 BC) – are among the impressive finds at the necropolis in Tarquinia, the birthplace of Tarquinius Priscus, the legendary first king of Rome.

and decor. The vast necropolis complex partly resembles an underground city, with streets and courtyards. The tombs at Tarquinia, mostly still in the necropolis are best known for their frescoes depicting banquets, dancing, and hunting scenes. They all date from the 6th to the 2nd century BC.

Lake Bracciano, known as Lacus Sabatinus in ancient times, lies 50 km (31 miles) north-west of the Roman city center. The almost circular crater lake – the caldera or basin from the Sabatino volcano that became extinct around 330,000 years ago – is surrounded by the Sabatine Mountains.

Hot mineral springs on the lake's shores confirm its volcanic origins. For the Romans, the lake is a superb sports and leisure facility in the midst of beautiful countryside; it also serves as the water reservoir, which feeds the restored Sabatine water duct of Trajan, the Acqua Paola, which supplies

On the north shore of Lake Bracciano (top right) lies Trevignano Romano, a town that was probably already settled in Etruscan times, as nearby necropolises suggest. Trevignano Romano is dominated by a castle built on the orders of Pope Innocent III between 1198 and 1268 (large picture).

Trastevere and the Vatican with water. Both this lake and Lago di Martignano, directly adjacent to it, were included in the Parco Naturale Regionale di Bracciano-Martignano in 1999. There are three cities on the lake's shores: Bracciano, Anguillara Sabazia, and Trevignano Romano.

THE ROMAN COUNTRYSIDE AND THE SEA

Ostia Antica, the trading and naval port of ancient Rome, was built in the 4th and 3rd centuries BC. Excavations revealed that the city flourished for many centuries with magnificent houses, markets, public baths, taverns, sports complexes, and a playhouse. Its population was about 100,000 but was decimated by several malaria epidemics. The gradual silting up of the port through material carried by the Tiber River, which empties here contributed to its decline and it was abandoned in the 9th century. However the old town's ancient buildings, and magnificent frescoes are well worth

In the last few decades the charm of the Lido di Ostia, around 25 km (15 miles) south of Rome, had somewhat faded, but today visitors from the capital still enjoy the baths (top right), discos, and bars. The ancient theater (large picture; above: a detail) on the excavation site of Ostia Antica dates from the time of Emperor Augustus. Originally it could seat around 3,000 spectators.

visiting. This process also led to the construction of modern Ostia: the site of Lido di Ostia or "Rome Beach" was once open sea. Work began on reclaiming coastal land in 1883 and modern Ostia was founded in 1908. A motorway was built in 1927, which links the resort and the capital.

Castel Gandolfo is a small town on the edge of a crater lake in the Colli Albani (Alban Hills), on the site of the ancient city of Alba Longa, founded some time after 1150 BC and destroyed by the Romans. Castel Gandolfo is best known for being the papal summer residence. The Catholic Church purchased the castello towards the end of the 16th century. Urban VIII (real name Maffeo Barberini, pope 1623–1644), already enjoyed spending his time here when he was still a cardinal, and after Carlo Maderno had enlarged and renovated the castle with the help of the prominent architects Bartolo-

Alongside the papal palace (top right) which included the Vatican Observatory from 1933 to 2008, the papal estate at Castel Gandolfo also comprises the adjacent Villa del Moro and Villa Cybo. Altogether the terrain, which is officially an "extraterritorial possession of the Holy See" covers 55 ha (124 acres), making it 11 ha (27 acres) larger then the Vatican State itself. About half of this is taken up by gardens (large picture).

meo Breccioli and Domenico Castelli, he became the first pope to spend his vacation at the peaceful residence in 1626. The Pontifical Villas of Castel Gandolfo comprise about 55 ha (124 acres) and the extensive grounds are divided into beautiful formal gardens as well as open farm land.

Located a short way north of Castel Gandolfo is Frascati, known for the crisp white wine of the same name. It was a holiday resort for the Roman young, rich, and beautiful in ancient times. In the Renaissance the village became one of the Castelli Romani, a region formed by 16 hill towns between 20 and 53 km (12.5 to 33 miles) from Rome or in the Alban Hills. Two routes take visitors into this area characterized by gently rolling hills, a mild climate, and natural water sources: the ancient Via Appia and the medieval Via Tuscolana. Here you'll find aqueducts and mausoleums.

Another distinctive feature is the palaces of Roman nobility, which were often enlarged into fortresses in the Middle Ages. One of the most attractive palaces in Frascati is the Villa Aldobrandini. The present building dates from the early 17th century, while the imposing façade is 18th century.

Fountains and water features (large picture and above) decorate the gardens of the Villa Aldobrandini (top). Located south-east of the Piazza Marconi in Frascati it is also known as Belvedere. The villa was built between 1598 and 1604 as a country residence for Cardinal Pietro Aldobrandini, the nephew and right hand of Pope Clement VIII – a position that was given its own title in the Papal States at the time: "cardinal-nephew".

THE ROMAN COUNTRYSIDE AND THE SEA

Cardinal Ippolito d'Este, a member of the famous ruling dynasty from Ferrara and the son of Lucrezia Borgia, chose a former Benedictine monastery in Tivoli as his residence in 1550. Some rooms in the palace were embellished with beautiful frescoes in the Roman Mannerism style by Livio Agresti and Federico Zuccari. On the slopes below the villa, Ippolito d'Este had a park set out by Pirro Ligorio and Alberto Galvani, featuring a widely branched system of fountains and water features: the "garden of miracles", where countless fountains cascade into thousands of

small streams. His successor, Cardinal Alessandro d'Este, re-designed the park in 1605. The architect, Bernini later helped with the construction work – the Fontana del Bicchierone is attributed to him. The Organo Idraulico water organ is the masterpiece of the French designer, Claude Venard.

After a period of decline, Villa d'Este (large picture: the Salone della Fontana; above: the depiction of a Tiburtine Sibyl) was renovated from 1851 under Cardinal Gustav von Hohenlohe and became a society gathering point, where, among others, Franz Liszt liked to stay while composing. The park with its more than 500 fountains, water features, and water spouts (top) became a model for water gardens all over Europe.

THE ROMAN COUNTRYSIDE AND THE SEA

Publius Aelius Hadrianus, the 14th emperor of Rome from 117 to 138, was an arts lover and enjoyed visiting countries in his Empire, especially Greece and Egypt. On his initiative many spectacular new buildings were erected: the Pantheon and the Castello di Angelo in Rome and Hadrian's town in Athens. He also had Hadrian's Wall built in Britain. His own residence was southwest of Tivoli, and built in 118 to 134. The complex, covering around 120 ha (300 acres), is an enlargement of an older villadating from the 1st century BC, and resembles an imperial garden town rather

At the Teatro Marittimo (large picture) a grand colonnaded hall surrounded a giant water basin which had an island in the middle – this was the emperor's refuge where he liked to paint, his favorite pastime. The vast complex also comprises the copy of an Egyptian canal or *canopus* (above). Located around 30 km (19 miles) northwest of Rome, the villa is integrated into the countryside around Tivoli (top right).

than a traditional country residence. The structures are mostly copies of Greek buildings, and follow the natural layout of the land. The magnificent complex includes fountains, lakes, temples, baths and beautiful gardens and is a shining model of the skill and imagination of the architects of that period.

Out and about on a motor scooter – that's the epitomy of the
Roman way of life, even if the
traffic on the roads in the city is
mostly rather chaotic.

COMPACT ROME

The city of la dolce vita, the focal point of Christianity, the Eternal City: the capital of the former Roman Empire and of Italy is many things to many people. The city on the Tiber boasts a wealth of churches, palaces, museums, and ancient monuments, romantic historic districts and idyllic hilly surroundings in the countryside between the Apennines and the Tyrrhenian Sea. Rome is also a very fast-paced, lively, modern city, with first-class shops, excellent restaurants, and many opportunities for excursion to chic destinations. And in the Vatican City, it is also home to the smallest independent state in the world.

COMPACT ROME

The Ara Pacis Augustae can be seen within an impressive complex of museums. It gives an insight into the art of sculpting in ancient times.

MUSEUMS, MUSIC, DRAMA

Ara Pacis The great Altar of Peace of Emperor Augustus was dedicated in 19 BC and has many finely sculpted reliefs in white marble. It is now protected under a shell designed by the architect Richard Meier.
Lungotevere in Augusta,
Tel 06 82 05 91 27,
www.arapacis.it,
Tues–Sun 9.00–19.00.

Galleria Colonna In the sumptuous apartments on the Palazzo Colonna is the extensive collection of paintings and sculptures assembled by the Colonna family. It includes works by masters such as Tintoretto, Annibale Carracci, Rubens, Pietro da Cortona, Anthony van Dyck, and many others.
Via Pilotta 17,
Tel 06 678 43 50,
www.galleriacolonna.it,
Sat 9.00–13.00.

Galleria dell'Accademia Nazionale di San Luca The academy promotes painting, sculpture, and architecture; the gallery has over 500 portraits and numerous other paintings and sculptures, including superb works by Canova, Raphael, Rubens, and van Dyck.
Piazza dell'Accademia di San Luca 77,
Tel 06 679 88 48,
www.accademiasanluca.it,
Mon–Sat 9.00–13.00.

Galleria Doria Pamphilj The private collection of the Pamphili family, which was started in 1650, boasts significant works by Titian, Caravaggio, Annibale Carracci, Velázquez, Claude Lorrain, Pieter Brueghel the Elder, and others.
Piazza del Collegio Romano 1a,
Tel 06 679 73 23,
www.doriapamphilj.it,
Fri–Wed 10.00–17.00.

Galleria Spada This collection housed in the Palazzo Spada and including antiquities and paintings by Titian, Reni, Guercino, and Gentileschi, among others was acquired by Cardinal Bernardino Spada. It is now owned by the state. The Galleria Prospettiva, a peristyle by Francesco Borromini in the palace courtyard, is also well worth a visit.
Piazza Capo di Ferro 3,
Tel 06 686 11 58,
www.beniculturalionline.it,
Mon–Sun 9.00–19.00.

Museo Barracco Located in a 16th-century palace designed by Antonio da Sangallo the Younger, these ancient works of art from around the Mediterranean area were collected by Giovanni Barracco.
Corso Vittorio Emanuele II 168, Tel 06 68 80 68 48,
www.museobarracco.it,
Tues–Sun 9.00–19.00.

Ancient sculptures on display at the Museo Barracco.

Museo di Keats e Shelley Near the Spanish Steps, in a former artists' quarter, this museum is dedicated to the poet John Keats, who died here in 1821, aged 25, of tuberculosis. It also contains the ashes and mementoes of Shelley and Lord Byron.
Piazza di Spagna 26,
Tel 06 678 42 35,
www.keats-shelley-house.org,
Mon–Fri 9.00– 13.00 and
15.00–18.00, Sat 11.00–14.00
and 15.00–18.00.

Museo Nazionale Etrusco di Villa Giulia Founded in 1889 and housed in a mannerist villa, this museum has superb Etruscan objects, as well as an important collection of Greek vases.
Piazzale Villa Giulia 9,
Tel 06 320 19 51,
www.archeologia.
beniculturali.it,
Tues–Sun 8.30–19.30.

Museo Nazionale delle Paste Alimentari What would Rome and Italy be without pasta! This museum explains all about the history, production technology, and nutritional values of the national dish.
Piazza Scanderbeg 117,
Tel 06 699 11 19,
9.30–17.30, daily.

FESTIVALS AND EVENTS

Natale di Roma The founding of the city of Rome is celebrated at different locations throughout the city, but the main part of the activities takes place at the Piazza del Campidoglio. Bands play, and people in historical costumes re-enact scenes from the city's history. The festivities conclude with a magnificent firework display.
Tel 06 51 60 79 51,
www.gsr-roma.com,
19–21 April.

Opera summer season at the Teatro dell'Opera The impressive ruins of the Caracalla Baths form the open-air backdrop for the opera summer festival.
Teatro dell'Opera,
Tel 06 48 16 01,
www.operaroma.it,
end Jun–Aug.

SPORT, GAMES, FUN

City tours on bus 110 If you are new to Rome and want to gain a first impression of its highlights and overall layout, a good starting point is a trip on the 110, the open-top sightseeing bus. The tour starts near the Termini station and there are ten stops at which you can get off. If you remain on the bus, the tour takes two hours. Piazza del Cinquecento in front of the Termini Station,
Tel 06 684 09 01,
www.trambusopen.com, daily.

Annibale Gammarelli is the personal tailor to popes and other church dignitaries.

HEALTH AND BEAUTY

Tevere Village Sun-lovers need not miss out in the heart of the city. With a fantastic view of St. Peter's, this is a good spot right by the Tiber, between the Piazza Navona and the Castel Sant'Angelo, in which to hire a sun lounger and parasol. There are swimming pools for cooling off.

SHOPPING

Angelo Vitti Atelier Angelo Vitti's exclusive designs for women are on sale in this shop situated not far from the Spanish Steps and the Palazzo del Quirinale. Good shopping for those with bulging wallets.
Via Gregoriana 45/46,
Tel 06 678 08 20,
www.angelovitti.it

Annibale Gammarelli This somewhat unassuming tailor's shop has been exclusively responsible for supplying the pope's robes for over 200 years. It also produces distinguished clerical vestments.
Via di Santa Chiara 34,
Tel 06 68 80 13 14.

Enoteca Buccone A legendary wine, champagne, vinegar, and oil shop located in a former stable block. Selection is made easier if you have fortified yourself with one of the small, tasty snacks on offer first.
Via Ripetta 19/20,
Tel 06 361 21 54,
www.enotecabuccone.com,
Mon–Thurs midday, Fri, Sat
midday and evenings.

Fanshop AS Roma As the finances of football club Associazione Sportiva Roma could do with a boost, this shop hopes to add to the contents of its coffers by selling the usual club paraphernalia, as well as tickets for the "Giallorossi" (yellow-red) matches.
Piazza Colonna 360,
Tel 06 678 65 14,
www.asromastore.it

Ferrari Fanshop Everything to do with Ferrari, one of Italy's national institutions, and its iconic and (generally) red Italian sports car. The only things you can't buy here are the cars themselves.
Via Tomacelli 147,
Tel 06 689 29 79, www.
romecity.it/Ferraristore.htm,
Mon–Sat 10.00–19.30, Sun
from 11.00.

The Lion Bookshop Founded in 1947, this bookstore has over 30,000 titles in English on its shelves, covering fiction and non-fiction, for adults and children, and with in-depth specialist sections. The atmosphere is friendly and there is a small café serving bagels, cookies,

Motor sports fans and Ferrari fanatics find all that the heart desires at the Ferrari Fanshop.

and cakes. It is situated close to the Spanish Steps and the Piazza del Popolo.
Via dei Greci 36, Tel 06 3265 4007/06 3265 0437, www.thelionbookshop.com

La Cicogna A shopping paradise for mothers and expectant mums with cash to spare. Maternity fashion and a large selection of somewhat extravagant children's clothes, not necessarily for everyday use, are available. There are usually some items at reduced prices at "The Stork" (la cicogna).
Via Frattina 138, Tel 06 679 19 12.

La Soffitta sotto i Portici A monthly market with paintings, graphic art, engravings, ceramics, and porcelain, as well as secondhand items, clocks, and furniture. There are around 100 stalls to search for bargains.

Piazza Augusto Imperatore, every third Sunday in the month; 10.00 until dusk.

Max Mara The Italian outlet of a well-known women's fashion chain. The sales assistants are friendly, there's a wide range of clothing, and the prices are reasonable. Achille Maramotti founded his ready-to-wear empire in Rome in 1951.
Via Frattina 28, Tel 06 679 36 38.

Mercato delle Stampe A market with an enormous selection of antiquarian and art books, as well as good-quality prints and engravings.
Piazza Borghese, Mon–Fri 9.00–17.30, Sat, Sun 9.00–19.00, closed Aug.

Mercato di Piazza delle Coppelle A photogenic and lively fruit, vegetable, and flower market close to the Pantheon.

Piazza delle Coppelle, Mon–Sat 7.00–13.00.

Only Hearts American designer Jean Frances Ottaviano has three shops in Rome – the only city in Europe in which she has a base – selling original and unusual fashion at reasonable prices. Underwear, bags, and T-shirts are in particular demand.
Piazza della Chiesa Nuova, Tel 06 686 46 47, www.onlyhearts.com, Tues–Sat 10.00–20.00, Sun–Mon 12.00–20.00.

Salvatore Ferragamo The finest leather purses, bags, and ladies' and men's shoes on sale in two almost adjacent shops. Italian shoe designer Salvatore Ferragamo who founded the company began his career producing *scarpe belle* (beautiful shoes) for film productions in Hollywood in the 1920s.

Salvatore Ferragamo, world-famous designer of shoes and clothing, has a store in the Via Condotti.

Via Condotti 65 and 73/74, Tel 06 678 11 30 and Tel 06 679 15 65, www.salvatoreferragamo.it

EATING AND DRINKING

Cinque Lune A popular small pasticceria, with a wonderful selection of pastries, near the Piazza Navona.
Corso del Rinascimento, Tel 06 880 10 05, Tues–Sun 8.00–21.30.

Ditirambo Close to the Campo de' Fiori, this restaurant serves creative Roman cuisine using the freshest ingredients. The pasta, bread, and desserts are all homemade.
Piazza della Cancellaria 74, Tel 06 87 16 26, www.ristoranteditirambo.com

Enoteca Cul de Sac Excellent Roman cuisine and an enormous selection of top wines.

Piazza Pasquino 73, Tel 06 58 33 39 20.

Hard Rock Café Rome A Roman outpost of the famous international restaurant chain; dine in a room decorated with all kinds of rock memorabilia – guitars, stage clothing, photographs, and gold records.
Via Vittorio Veneto 62 a/b, Tel 06 420 30 51, www.hardrock.com, Restaurant: Sun–Thurs 12.00–24.00, Fri–Sat 12.00–1.00; bar: Sun–Thurs 12.00–1.30, Fri–Sat 12.00–2.00.

Il Margutta One of the best and most sophisticated vegetarian restaurants to open in Rome for 30 years. And it's not just the meals that are delicious – the locally grown organic wines are too. On Saturdays, a live band plays, and there's a jazz band on the last Tuesday of the month.

Via Margutta 118, Tel 06 32 65 05 77, www.ilmargutta.it, 12.30–15.30 and 1 9.30–23.30, daily.

La Penna d'Oca A snug, sophisticated restaurant offering some outstanding dishes. Located just south of Piazza del Popolo and a bit secluded.
Via della Penna 53, Tel 06 320 28 98.

La Rosetta Founded in 1966, and highly praised in the Italian press, this family-run fish restaurant near the Pantheon is the best of its kind in Rome, perhaps even the best in Italy. The dishes have a Sicilian slant, often simple but extremely delicious. The fish is freshly caught from the waters off the ports of Lazio, Anzio, Civitavecchia, and Terracina. Smart dress and reservations are expressly requested.

Roman cooking and good wine can be enjoyed at the Ditirambo.

Via della Rosetta 8,
Tel 06 86 10 02,
www.larosetta.com,
Mon–Sat lunch and dinner.

Le Jardin de Russie Perhaps the most beautiful five-star hotel in the city, Hotel de Russie boasts a first-class restaurant with beautiful terraced gardens. The Mediterranean and international cuisine makes the most of the excellent local produce on offer.
Via del Babuino 9,
Tel 06 32 88 88 70,
www.hotelderussie.it,
7.00–10.30, 12.30–14.30 and 19.30–22.30, daily.

L'Orso 80 A pleasant restaurant with a good selection of antipasti and delicious meat, fish, and pasta dishes – all at reasonable prices.
Via dell'Orso 33,
Tel 06 86 49 04,
www.orso80.it

Nino A classic Italian restaurant located near the Spanish Steps, with a charming atmosphere and a Tuscan slant. Much frequented by the Romans themselves – and sometimes by movie stars such as Jennifer Lopez, Brooke Shields, and Jim Carrey among others, who joined celebrity couple Tom Cruise and Katie Holmes to celebrate their wedding here.
Via Borgognona 11,
Tel 06 678 67 52.

ACCOMMODATION

Casa Howard Rome pulses with life around the Spanish Steps, and though the two beautiful Casa Howard boutique hotels are close by, they are still a relatively well-kept secret. The Via Capo le Case hotel, opened in 2000, was carefully created with great attention to detail by owner Jenifer Howard Forneris. Interior designer Tommaso Ziffer, who also made his mark in the Hotel de Russie, has created a stylish hotel at Via Sistina. You can spoil yourself and have breakfast served in your room, and after a strenuous day sightseeing, the small Turkish bath offers gentle relaxation for tired muscles.
Via Capo le Case 18 and Via Sistina149,
Tel 06 69 92 45 55,
www.casahoward.com

De Russie A high-class hotel located not far from the Spanish Steps and the Piazza del Popolo, with a highly recommended gourmet restaurant, a stylish spa, and a beautifully laid out garden. An oasis of wellbeing in the very heart of the Eternal City.
Via del Babuino 9,
Tel 06 32 88 81,
www.hotelderussie.it

The Hassler Villa Medici luxury hotel is located in an enviable position in the heart of Rome: above the Spanish Steps.

Eden This top international hotel in a traditional style is one of the best addresses in Rome. The rooms and suites are luxuriously furnished with antiques and fine marble baths – politicians and well-known Italian stage stars are among the regular clientele. The view from the roof terrace is simply stunning. The La Terrazza restaurant is considered one of the best in the city, but, unsurprisingly, the prices are correspondingly high.
Via Ludovisi 49,
Tel 06 47 81 21,
www.hotel-eden.it

Hassler Villa Medici A first-class hotel, in a superb location just above the Spanish Steps. The interior and facilities are appropriately luxurious: marble baths and antiques are a feature of the comfortable rooms, and the service is excellent as one would expect. The

Hassler is also the much-loved residence of the Swedish royal couple (which is why it has the Queen Silvia Suite). The hotel also boasts a good restaurant as well as an incomparable view over one of the most beautiful squares in Rome.
Piazza Trinità dei Monti 6,
Tel 06 69 93 40,
www.hotelhasslerroma.com

Hotel d'Inghilterra One of the traditional hotels, dating from the 16th century it served as a guesthouse for the nearby Palazzo Torlonia. The venerable hotel is rightly proud of its famous past guests such as John Keats, Ernest Hemingway, Franz Liszt, and Oscar Wilde. This dignified hotel is an excellent base for visiting the old historic heart of the city as well as for extended shopping expeditions in the elegant Via Condotti.
Via Bocca di Leone 14,

Tel 06 69 98 11,
www.hotelinghilterraroma.it

Navona This small hotel situated in a 15th-century palazzo, just off the Corso del Rinascimento, is an ideal base from which to explore the city for sightseeing by day or strolling at night. The simple yet comfortable rooms are located on the first floor.
Via dei Sediari 8,
Tel 06 68 66 42 03,
www.hotelnavona.com

Portoghesi This old house was converted into a small hotel about 150 years ago, but today it offers all the usual modern facilities. Located close to the Piazza Navona, in the very heart of the city, it is an ideal starting point for sightseeing or walks. It's worth staying here for the view from the roof terrace alone – ideal for your snaps of Rome.

The Raphael also accommodates celebrities among its guests, for example, the Hollywood star Julia Roberts.

Via dei Portoghesi 1,
Tel 06 686 42 31,
www.hotelportoghesiroma.it

Raphael Located just a few steps from the lively Piazza Navona, the Raphael is one of the most sophisticated hotels in the city. The charming façade is ivy-clad and the interior is decorated with numerous paintings, antiques, and sculptures. The rooms on the third floor of the hotel were designed by architect Richard Meier, using the finest materials and fitted with the latest sound systems. The restaurant pampers its guests with a selection of superb dishes, served on attractive hand-painted plates. Plus you can enjoy the stunning view from the roof terrace. Stop by for a glass of prosecco and experience it for yourself.
Largo Febo 2,
Tel 06 68 28 31,
www.raphaelhotel.com

NIGHTLIFE

Gilda This large, well-known club is a meeting point for chic Romans and international VIPs alike. Here you can spot politicians, actors, film stars, and sport stars dining and dancing. There are several rooms and the club is divided into a disco and a bar. You need to be smartly dressed in order to in; but entry is often by formal invitation only. Best to know a regular.
Via Mario de' Fiori 97,
Tel 06 678 48 38,
www.midra.it/website/
gilda/homepage.asp

New Open Gate Start your Roman night out here, with a dance followed by a choice cocktail or two at the bar of this popular disco.
Via San Nicola da Talentino,
Tel 06 482 44 64,
closed Sun and July–Sept.

Supperclub A great and really unusual club with a unique ambience, located in an ancient villa. Enjoy your nightlife ancient Roman style – eat and drink while reclining on sofas, just as they did in the days of the emperors. The music, however, is contemporary.
Via de' Nari 14,
Tel 06 68 80 72 07,
www.supperclub.com,
19.00–3.00, daily.

Zest Bar A meeting place for the beautiful people, this bar is located on the top floor of the Radisson Es Hotel, with superb panoramic views over the city and the nearby main station, Stazione Termini. Italian celecan be spotted here if you're lucky. On hot summer evenings, you can cool off with a quick dip in the pool on the roof terrace.
Via Filippo Turati 171,
Tel 06 44 48 41.

A performance of Giuseppe Verdi's *Nabucco* in the Caracalla Baths during the Estate Romana.

MUSEUMS, MUSIC, DRAMA

Forum Romanum When the Rome ruled the world, the orum Romanum, with its squares and buildings, was considered the "navel of the world", and is even visible as such with its round base. Before walking around the extensive ruins, climb the south side of the Capitoline Hill from where you can get a wonderful overview of the whole complex. The main entrances are at Piazza Santa Maria Nova near the Coliseum and the Largo Romolo e Remo. Avoid midday during high summer when the site sizzles in the hot sun.
Tel 06 699 01 10 or
Tel 06 39 96 77 00,
9.00 until 1 hour before
sunset, daily.

The Coliseum A stay in Rome has to include a visit to the Coliseum, the largest ancient structure in the city, even if the entry charges are not exactly cheap (there is a combined ticket with entrance to the Palatine Hill). The site is spectacular and breathtakingly large, particularly if you decide to climb up to the upper circles of the arena. The Coliseum could once hold 50,000 spectators and at a push and shove even 75,000. Rent one of the audio guides available in several languages, make use of a human *cicerone* (guide) – provided by the state and by private travel guide companies and let the architectural history be brought to life – or just wander around this great building and soak up the atmosphere of one of the world's most famous structures.
Piazza del Colosseo,
Tel 06 39 96 77 00 oder
Tel 06 700 54 69, 9.00 until
1 hour before sunset, daily,
or until 16.30 in winter.

Notte Bianca Similar to the *nuits blanches* or "white nights" of Paris, Rome too makes a night into day at the beginning of September each year. Museums, galleries, and some public building are all open to the general public for free. There are concerts in many places aorund town and the bars also stay open all night. Art and culture, free for all.
www.lanottebianca.it,
im Sept.

FESTIVALS AND EVENTS

Caracalla Baths On warm summer nights the caldarium becomes an open-air stage for opera performances by the Teatro dell'Opera. Opera connoisseurs may find fault with the acoustics, but as a unique experience, when beautiful music fills the night sky in a magical ancient setting, it cannot be faulted.

The Ethiopian runner Firehiwot Dado won the 16th, the Marathon of Rome, on 21 March 2010 (2:25:28).

Via delle Terme di Caracalla, Tel 06 361 10 64 and Tel 06 48 16 01, www.operaroma.it

Estate Romana In the summer months, Rome becomes a spectacular setting for a variety of events held in its squares, palaces, villas, gardens, and parks – from concerts, and cabarets, to drama and cinema. The city's monuments are illuminated atmospherically and musicians and entertainers perform in the streets, alleys, and squares, when the whole of the old city is transformed into an open-air stage. *Information and schedule: Tel 06 497 11, www.romaturismo.com, www.estateromna. commune.roma.it, mi- June–end Sept.*

Easter On Good Friday, the ceremonial Via Crucis (Way of the Cross) procession by torchlight, led by the pope, winds its way around the Coliseum, passing through the 14 Stations of the Cross established by Pope Benedict XIV in 1749. The procession is a reminder of Christ's last walk to Golgotha.

SPORT, GAMES, FUN

Maratona Like many other cities, Rome also stages a marathon. The participants are challenged to a tough 42.195-km (26.2-mile) race around the city, to cheering crowds. *www.maratonadiroma.it, late March.*

SHOPPING

Alberta Gloves While gloves are worn less these days as a simple fashion accessory, they remain a necessity in colder climates in winter. This shop carries numerous styles in every size and material, and for every conceivable occasion, with the exception of gloves required for manual work. *Corso Vittorio Emanuele II 18, Tel 06 678 57 53.*

La Chiave Ethnic odds and ends from all over the world at low prices, and more unusual objects for the home: crockery, dream catchers, lamps, furniture, and much more. *Largo delle Stimmate 28, Tel 06 68 30 88 48.*

Rinascita A book and record store that stocks a good selection of world music, jazz, blues, and classical recordings. Plus tickets for gigs. *Villa delle Botteghe oscure 5, Tel 06 69 92 24 36.*

Sciù Scià Group di Biaggi Bruno A tiny little shop selling handmade women's shoes stacked in boxes, in both classic

One of the classics of Roman cuisine: spaghetti alla carbonara.

and contemporary styles. Time spent rummaging here is time well spent.
Via di Torre Argentina 8,
Tel 06 68 80 67 77.

Galleria Alberto Sordi The trendy shopping mall in the heart of Rome was built in 1914 and offers much more than fashonable clothes: it also houses the Feltrinelli music and book store as well as a café.
Piazza Colonna 31–35,
Tel 06 85 35 54 31
Mon–Sat 8.30/9.00–12.30/13
and 15.30/16.00–19.30/20.00
(closed Aug.).

EATING AND DRINKING

L'Insalata Ricca How about trying something other than pasta for lunch? The salads here are refreshing, fresh, varied, and have interesting combinations, but are not too heavy on either the stomach or the wallet. They also have a selection of pasta, pizza, meat, and fish dishes too. One of 12 branches in this chain.
Largo die Chiavari 85,
Tel 06 85 68 80 36,
www.linsalataricca.it,
12.00–16.00 and
19.00–24.00, daily.

La Piazzetta A pleasant gay- and lesbian-friendly restaurant, located in a little alleyway a short way the north of the Coliseum. The starters, main dishes, and desserts from the buffet are all excellent.
Vicolo del Buon Consiglio
23 a, Tel 06 699 16 40,
Mon–Sat.

Quelli della Taverna A traditional local taverna near the Teatro Argentina, serving wonderful, hearty starters and main dishes that are really simple but all the tastier for that. Prices are good too.

Via dei Barbieri 25,
Tel 06 686 96 60.

Renato e Luisa A modern trattoria with a penchant for French cuisine, situated near the Torre Argentina. The service can be a little indifferent, but if that doesn't put you off, you can experience some real culinary delights here.
Via dei Barbieri 25,
Tel 06 686 96 60,
www.renatoeluisa.it,
Tues–Sun 8.30–24.30.

Vecchia Roma This well-established restaurant has an attractive terrace and is often frequented by high-ranking politicians and celebrities. It has been owned by the Palladino family since 1870. Vecchia Roma serves classic Italian and local Roman cuisine. The pasta, risotto, and polenta dishes, and the diverse antipasti are always delicious.

Try some Antipasti Tricolore and enjoy the delicious culinary treasures of Italy.

Piazza Campitelli 18,
Tel 06 96 86 46 04,
Thurs–Tues, closed Aug.

ACCOMMODATION

Forum A good, mid-range hotel situated behind the Imperial Forums. In fine weather, it is worth visiting the restaurant on the roof terrace, from where there is a great view.
Via Tor de' Conti 25 ,
Tel 06 679 24 46,
www.hotelforumrome.com

Hotel dei Gladiatori This hotel is in an impressive position opposite one of Rome's main sights, the world-famous Coliseum. Although the traffic never stops at all, the view of the arena is fabulous, particularly from the hotel's beautiful roof terrace.
Via Labicana 125,
Tel 06 77 59 13 80,
www.hotelgladiatori.com

Nerva An ideal base from which to explore the sites of ancient Rome, this hotel is situated close to the Roman Forum. The 19 rooms are both quiet despite the central location and comfortable.
Via Tor de' Conti 3,
Tel 06 679 37 64,
www.hotelnerva.com

Perugia A small, simple, and reliably run hotel, not far from the Coliseum. The prices are reasonable for a hotel in such a central position.
Via del Colosseo 7,
Tel 06 679 72 00,
www.hotel-perugia.romaviva.com

Richmond Just a few steps from the hotel you will reach all the ancient monuments and the best of the lively shopping streets, this hotel is owned by the Gnecco family, who pride themselves on impeccable ser-vice. The rooms are comfortable and well-furnished, and there is also a beautiful roof terrace, where you can break-fast in summer while enjoying the fantastic view of the Impe-rial Forums.
Largo C. Ricci 36,
Tel 06 69 94 12 56,
www.hotelrichmondroma.com

Teatro di Pompeo A good hotel with a simple façade built on truly historic founda-tions: it stands on a section of the spectators' stand of the Teatro di Pompeo, the theater built by Pompey during his second consulship and ope-ned in 55 BC. There are remains of the old ruins throughout the hotel, and breakfast is taken in a room with ancient Roman vaulting.
Largo del Pallaro 8,
Tel 06 68 30 01 70,
www.hotelteatrodipompeo.it

Pope Benedict XVI blesses the crowds during Urbi et Orbion Easter Sunday 2010.

MUSEUMS, MUSIC, DRAMA

Castel Sant'Angelo The mausoleum of Emperor Hadrian and his family, later used as a fortress and refuge by the Roman Catholic popes, has a remarkable frescoed interior and a museum displaying weapons, furniture, and fascinating objects from everyday life.
Lungotevere Castello 50,
Tel 06 681 91 11,
www.castelsantangelo.com,
Tues–Sun 9.00–19.00.

Museo Storico Artistico Tesoro di San Pietro This has liturgical items, fragments from papal tombs and ancient sarcophagi.
St Peter's Sacristy, left-hand aisle; summer: 9.00.

FESTIVALS AND EVENTS

The Easter blessing The highpoint of the Easter celebrations in the Vatican is the *urbi et orbi* blessing ("to the city and to the world"), given by the Holy Father at midday on Easter Sunday to those on St. Peter's Square or in front of their television sets.
Vatikan/Petersplatz,
Easter Sunday.

SHOPPING

Angelo di Nepi Italian designer fashion meets Bollywood: Nepi links two completely different worlds of fashion and uses the finest fabrics and elaborate embroidery to make his creations, which have a hint of the exotic.
Via Cola di Rienzo 267 a,
Tel 06 322 48 00,
www.angelodinepi.it

Castroni If you should tire of the traditional Italian fare such as prosciutto and pasta, espresso and grappa, this delicatessen stocks international ingredients galore, which are not available almost anywhere else in Rome – from corned beef, to hundreds of different varieties of teas. There's also an irresistible selection of international sweets.
Via Cola di Rienzo 196,
Tel 06 687 43 83,
www.castroni.com,
Mon–Sat 8.00–20.00.

Doctor Music A little music store, with a great selection of rock and pop, country rock, blues, and jazz.
Via dei Gracchi 41/43,
Tel 06 320 05 43, Mon–Sat
9.30–13.00 and 16.00–20.00.

Enoteca Costantini A cozy and richly stocked wine cellar located opposite the Castel Sant'Angelo.
Piazza Cavour 16,
Tel 06 320 35 75,
www.pierocostantini.it,

Everyone will find the right drop for them at the inviting Enoteca Costantini. All the bottles are arranged by wine region.

Mon 16.30–20.00, Tues–Sat 9.00–13.00 and 16.30–20.00.

Euroclero This shop sells the garments worn by Roman Catholic men and women in their religious roles – from the simple habits for monks and nuns, to the more elaborate cassocks and vestments for priests, and not forgetting a good selection of "chaste" underwear. Candles and holy figures and images are also available.
Via Paolo VI 31,
Tel 06 68 80 17 22,
www.euroclero.it,
Mon–Fri 9.00–13.00 and 14.00–18.00, Sat 9.00–12.30.

Franchi Another alimentari (delicatessen) worth visiting, with an outstanding range of Italian cheeses, wines, hams, and salamis. Their ready-made snacks are also excellent.
Via Cola di Rienzo 200–204,
Tel 06 686 45 76

Mercato della Piazza dell'Unità A busy market hall located in the middle of the Prati district that sells everyday food as well as fine culinary treats. Cut flowers are also available.
Via Cola di Rienzo,
Mon–Sat 7.00–20.00.

EATING AND DRINKING

Benito e Gilberto al Falco A rather tiny restaurant that has been specializing exclusively in fish dishes for more than three decades now, and can claim some very famous customers. Fish and seafood, always freshly caught or harvested, are prepared simply and are invariably delicious. The wine list is extensive and the homemade desserts also come highly recommended.
Via del Falco 19,
Tel 06 686 77 69,
www.dabenitoegilberto.com,

Tues–Sat 12.30–15.00 and 19.45–23.30.

Del Frate An elegant wine bar, housed in brick vaults formerly used for storing wine. An ideal place in which to relax and satisfy any hunger pangs after a visit to the Vatican – unusual dishes at fair prices.
Via degli Scipioni 118,
Tel 06 323 64 37,
Mon–Sat 13.00–15.00 and 19.30–1.00, Sun 19.30–1.00, closed for two weeks in Aug.

Dino & Tony An original, convivial Roman trattoria, with red-checkered tablecloths, enormous portions, waiters who sing at times, are miserable at others, and even a few tables outside on the street. The antipasti alone are worth the visit.
Via Leone IV, 60,
Tel 06 39 73 32 84,
Mon–Sat 12.30–15.30 and from 19.30.

The interior of the Latteria di Borgo Pio is classically styled, the dishes and drinks on offer are always freshly cooked.

Faggiani The Faggiani Bar is certainly worth a visit for Italian snacks and a great breakfast if you're in the area. There's a good mix of people among the clientele. The cake shop next door is really something special, where you can get the best bread, cakes, and pastries in the whole city.
Via Giuseppe Ferrari 23,
Tel 06 39 73 97 42.

Gelateria Old Bridge Without doubt, one of the best ice-cream shops in Rome, and generally packed with people on sunny days. The portions are generous.
Via dei Bastioni di
Michelangelo 5,
Tel 06 39 72 30 26.

Girarrosto Toscano Tuscan cuisine in Rome? The traditional rivalries between the northern Italians and those living in the capital go back many cent-

uries, but the contrast works really well in this restaurant. Try the homemade pasta and the delicious meat dishes.
Via Germanico 56,
Tel 06 39 72 57 17,
Tues–Sun 12.30–15.00,
20.00–23.30, closed Mon
and three weeks in Aug.

Il Simposio di Costantini This restaurant serves a wide range of wines from Enoteca Costantini, accompanied by light or more substantial hot dishes. Or you can just order tasty nibbles such as cheese and salami in the wine bar.
Piazza Cavour 16,
Tel 06 320 35 75,
www.pierocostantini.it,
restaurant: Mon–Sat 12.30–
15.00 and 19.30–23.00;
wine bar: Mon–Sat 12.30–
15.00 and 18.00–23.00.

Latteria di Borgo Pio A traditional ice-cream parlor and

coffee shop with classic marble counters and tiled floor, which will transport you back to the swinging 1960s.
Via Borgo Pio 48,
Tel 06 68 80 39 55,
Mon–Sat 9.00–21.00,
closed Aug.

Osteria dell'Angelo This restaurant is a little way north of the Vatican, but is well worth a visit for its outstanding no-nonsense, traditional cuisine. The fixed-price menus are particularly good value. Word has got out, so it would be a good idea to make a reservation.
Via Giovanni Bettolo 24/26,
Tel 06 372 94 70,
Tues, Fri 13.00–14.30,
Mon–Sat 20.00–22.30.

Shanti A popular and pretty restaurant serving mildly spiced Pakistani and Indian dishes. Ideal when you need a change from pasta and pizzas.

The atmosphere is great at the Alexanderplatz Jazz Club. A bar and a restaurant take care of their customers' physical welfare.

Via Fabio Massimo 68,
Tel 06 324 49 22.

ACCOMMODATION

Columbus The Columbus is an ideal base for visitors to the Vatican, with a view of St. Peter's Basilica. Built as a palace, the building dates from the 16th century and it still retains an air of aristocratic charm.
Via della Conciliazone 33,
Tel 06 686 54 35,
www.hotelcolumbus.net

Farnese A beautiful villa in the Prati quarter, and now a quiet hotel, within easy walking distance of the Vatican.
Via A. Farnese 30,
Tel 06 321 25 53,
www.hotelfarnese.com

MONASTIC BEDS

Many visitors to Rome take advantage of the simple, peaceful, and economic overnight accommodation in one of the many monasteries and convents located throughout the city, though most operate a strict curfew at night. Santa Susanna is the American Catholic Church in Rome and its website includes a list of convents that welcome guests.
www.santasusanna.org/co-
mingToRome/convents.html
Tel: 06 42 01 45 54

Residenza Paolo VI The Residenza Paolo VI has been converted as a hotel and opened as recently as 2000, on the occasion of the Holy Year. The building is based inside a former Augustinian monastery. This luxurious four-star hotel benefits from its uniquely attractive location, directly on St. Peter's Square. Stay here and you can enjoy excellent views from the terrace while sipping an aperitif.
Via Paolo VI 29,
Tel 06 68 40 39 60,
www.residenzapaolovi.com

NIGHTLIFE

Alexanderplatz Jazz Club One of the oldest and most famous jazz clubs in Rome, Alexanderplatz plays host to both local and international musicians. There's also a bar and restaurant for guests.
Via Ostia 9,
Tel 06 39 74 21 71,
www.alexanderplatz.it,
from 20.00, concerts:
rom 22.00.

Fonclea Live music has been played in this club in the Prati district for more than 30 years. With restaurant and pub.
Via Crescenzio 82 a,
Tel 06 689 63 02,
www.fonclea.it,
9.00–2.00, concerts:
from 21.30.

The Sala Santa Cecilia in the auditorium of the Parco della Musica is said to be Euope's largest concert hall.

MUSEUMS, MUSIC, DRAMA

Accademia Nazionale di Santa Cecilia Established by a fraternity of musicians in the 16th century, this academy and music conservatory has a renowned symphony orchestra and is one of the oldest music institutions in the world.
Viale Pietro de Coubertin 34,
Tel 06 80 820 58,
www.santacecilia.it

Auditorium Parco della Musica An architecturally spectacular auditorium, with three concert halls, the Parco della Musica is the largest venue of its kind in Rome. One of its halls, the Sala Santa Cecilia, is the largest concert hall in Europe.
Viale Pietro de Coubertin,
Tel 06 80 24 12 81,
www.auditorium.com,
10.00–20.00, daily, guided
tours on Sat, Sun, and public
holidays 10.30–17.30.

Galleria Nazionale d'Arte Moderna e Contemporanea The collection features paintings and sculpture from the 19th and 20th centuries, with a focus on Italian art.
Viale delle Belle Arti 131,
Tel 06 32 29 82 21,
www.gnam.beniculturali.it,
Mon–Fri 10.00–14.00.

Museo Nazionale degli Strumenti Musicali This specialist museum, with over 3,000 exhibits, gives an overview of the history and development of musical instruments.
Piazza S. Croce in Gerusalemme 9 a, Tel 06 328 10,
www.museostrumenti
musicali.it,
Tues–Sun 8.30–19.30.

Villa Torlonia The villa was once the private residence of Mussolini. Modern art and glass are exhibited. The park is open to the public.

Via Nomentana 70,
Tel 06 06 08, www.
museivillatorlonia.it,
Tues–Sun 9.00–19.00.

FESTIVALS AND EVENTS

Villa Celimontana Jazz Festival Experience a wide range of jazz styles in the gardens of the Villa Celimontana on summer evenings.
Villa Celimontana,
www.trovaromaonline.it,
June–Aug.

SPORT, GAMES, FUN

Acquasanta If you don't want to go without a round of golf even on vacation, then make sure you visit this elegant 18-hole course. It is located between Via Appia Nuova and Via Appia Antica and quite challenging. As an added benefit, as you swing the club, you can enjoy quite fabulous views of

Cinecittá: movie stills, posters, and other exhibits offer an insight into the work of the Roman film studios.

the Colli Albani and the aqueduct of Emperor Claudius.
Via Appia Nuova 716,
Tel 06 780 34 07,
www.golfroma.it

Campionato Ippico Internazionale The park of the Villa Borghese provides a fitting location for this major equestrian sporting event. The competitions take place on the Piazza di Siena, amid pine trees.
Tel 06 36 85 84 94 and
06 568 37 12,
www.piazzadisiena.com

Cinecittà Notable Italian directors such as Fellini, Pasolini, and Visconti shot some of their most famous films here.
Via Tuscolana 1055,
Tel 06 72 29 32 07,
www.cinecitta.com

Giardino Zoologico The zoo attempts to offer a habitat for the wild animals that is as close as possible to their original natural surroundings.
Piazzale del Giardino Zoologico (Villa Borghese),
8.30–17.30, daily,
in summer to 18.30.

Open-air cinema Watch a film under the stars with a gentle breeze wafting across the Tiber island, Isola Tiberina.
www.isoladelcinema.com,
mid June–mid Sept.

Teatro Mongiovino A puppet show in Rome's EUR district; the Marionette Museum next to the Teatro Mongiovino has over 400 puppets.
EUR, Via Giovanni Genocchi 15, Tel 06 513 94 05.

Swimming in the Olympic pool When Romans feel like a swim, they usually go to the beach, principally to the Lido di Ostia, but in the EUR district, you can cool off and also get some exercise in the Piscina delle Rose.
EUR, Viale America 20,
mid-June–mid-Sept 9.00–18.00, daily.

Stadio Olimpico The Olympic stadium is where Serie A football matches S.S. Lazio and AS Roma are held.
AS Roma: Tel 06 50 19 11,
www.asroma.it,
Lazio: Tel 06 32 37 33,
www.sslazio.it

HEALTH AND BEAUTY

Hammam la culla del benessere Relax and recuperate at these beautiful Turkish baths.
Via della Maratona 87,
Tel 06 36 29 85 73,
www.hammamroma.it,
Tues–Sun 12.00–21.00.

Sporting Palace Massages, a range of body treatments, and the standard fitness and cardio

The enthusiasm of the Roman Tifosi football fans knows no bounds – here the local match between AS Roma and Lazio.

equipment.. Plus there's a solarium a large swimming pool, and a hair salon.
Via Carlo Sigonio 21 a,
Tel 06 788 79 18,
www.sporting-palace.com,
Mon–Fri 9.30–22.30,
Sat 9.30–20.00.

SHOPPING

Mercatino di Ponte Milvio
Antiques, furniture, and crafts are traded at this market.
Lungotevere Coparati, 1st weekend of every month (Sat 15.00–19.00, Sun 8.00–19.00).

Mercato dell'Antiquariato di Piazza Verdi A flea market in the Villa Borghese area, with antiques, furniture, objets d'art, and reproductions.
Piazza Verdi, 4th Sunday of every month, 9.00–20.00.

Mercato di Testaccio A covered market, much loved by locals. The fruit and vegetable stands are a treat for the eyes as well as for the taste buds, and you can also buy shoes.
Piazza Testaccio,
Mon–Sat 7.30–13.30.

Volpetti A delicatessen that is well known throughout Rome; its olive oils, hams, and cheeses are highly recommended.
Via Marmorata 47,
Tel 06 574 23 52,
www.volpetti.com,
Mon–Sat 8.00–14.00,
Mon, Wed–Sat 17.00–20.15.

EATING AND DRINKING

Arancia Blu Relatively inexpensive vegetarian restaurant in the San Lorenzo quarter, with unusual and tasty dishes made from fresh ingredients. Great chocolate waffles
Via dei Latini 55,
Tel 06 445 41 05,
www.sanlorenzoroma.org

Delizie di Pizze Although relatively new, the Delizie di pizze has already acquired an excellent reputation.
Via Simeto 8–10,
8.00–15.00 and 16.30–21.00, daily.

La Pergola An award-winning restaurant in the Cavalieri Hilton Hotel, the best gourmet restaurant in Rome.
Via Cadlolo 101,
Tel 06 35 09 21 52,
www.cavalieri-hilton.it

Pommidoro Excellent pizzeria off the beaten tourist track, with a good atmosphere.
Piazza dei Sanniti 44,
Tel 06 445 26 92, Mon–Sat 12.00–16.00, 20.00–24.00.

ACCOMMODATION

Hotel Art by the Spanish Steps This chic designer hotel is located in the artists' district

The Volpettis have been traveling up and down the country for decades, always on the lookout for new delicacies.

of Via Margutta. With its clever use of lighting and mix of antique and modern furniture, it creates a special atmosphere.
Via Margutta 56,
Tel 06 32 87 11,
www.hotelart.it

Casa Internazionale delle Donne This international cultural center and women-only hotel is based in a 17th-century convent.
Via S. Francesco di Sales 1a,
Tel 06 68 40 17 24,
www.casainternazionale
delledonne.org

Cavalieri Hilton This large luxury hotel, part of the Hilton chain, is situated on the Monte Mario. Great panoramic views.
Via Cadlolo 101,
Tel 06 350 91,
www.cavalieri-hilton.it

Lord Byron A small hotel with all the comfort of a luxury one, in the quiet and charming vicinity of the Villa Borghese.
Via Giuseppe de Notaris 5, Tel 06 322 45 41,
www.lordbyronhotel.com

Radisson SAS Close to the main Termini station, the Radisson offers individually designed rooms with every comfort. The hotel has two restaurants, and a swimming pool on the roof terrace.
Via Filippo Turati 171,
Tel 06 44 48 41,
www.radisson.com/romeit

Sant'Anselmo Situated on the Aventine Hill, the Sant'Anselmo hotel lies in a small park with beautiful orange trees and is an oasis of calm.
Piazza di Sant'Anselmo 2,
Tel 06 57 00 57,
www.aventinohotels.com

Trastevere This small, inexpensive hotel makes an ideal base for an evening expedition through Trastevere. Plus apartments for families with children, or for small groups.
Via Luciano Manara 24,
Tel 06 581 47 13,
www.hoteltrastevere.net

NIGHTLIFE

Big Mama A long-established live music clublocated in Trastevere. Blues, jazz, and rock musicians have been appearing here since 1984.
Vicolo San Francesco a Ripa 18,
Tel 06 581 25 51,
www.bigmama.it,
21.00– 1.30, daily,
shows from 22.30.

Goa A club in the Ostiense quarter that features international DJs and also plays what's hot in Goa, India.
Via Giuseppe Libetta 13,
Tel 06 574 82 77,
Tues–Sun 23.00–4.00.

On the tracks of the ancient Etruscans – the Necropoli della Banditaccia located to the north-west of Cerveteri.

MUSEUMS, MUSIC, DRAMA

Cerveteri This town was once an important Etruscan city-state. It is now famous for several ancient necropolises, the highlight of which is the Necropoli della Banditaccia, located north-west of the town. In the middle of the town is a small Etruscan museum.
Necropoli della Banditaccia,
Tel 06 994 00 01,
Tues–Sun 8.30 until sunset.

Museo Nazionale di Cerveteri A 15th-century palazzo situated in the heart of the medieval town displays the art treasures that were discovered in the Etruscan graves found under the cliffs of Cerveteri and in the surrounding area. The finds from the necropolises date from the 9th to the 1st centuries BC, and they document the long history of this ancient settlement, which was known as Caere in ancient times. There are fascinating decorative bronze vessels from the Sorbo necropolis.
Piazza Santa Maria,
Tel 06 994 13 54,
Tues–Sun 8.30–18.30.

Frascati Famous for its wine, the town of Frascati has numerous grand villas from the Renaissance period. One of the villas, built for a Roman aristocrat, is the Villa Aldobrandini; set within a large park. It boasts beautiful 17th-century frescoes inside.
Frascati, Via Cardinal
Massaia 112, book in advance
Tel 06 942 93 31 (tourist
information center).

Ostia Antica Unlike other ancient sites, Ostia Antica has not been built over and Rome's former port is therefore exceptionally well preserved and today provides a fascinating glimpse into the lives of the ancient Romans. Visitors can see villas belonging to high-ranking patricians, multi-level tenements, baths, stages, artisans' studios, and shops. There are also public toilets.
Ostia, Scavi di Ostia,
Viale dei Romagnoli 717,
Tel 06 56 35 80 99,
Tues–Sun 8.30–16.00/18.00.

Museo Nazionale di Tarquinia This collection is housed in the attractive 15th-century Palazzo Vitelleschi. All the archeological finds come from the most important Etruscan center in Latium; they show how in the Etruscans world view life continued after death. Some particularly fine examples on display here are the painted friezes and a terracotta frieze with winged horses (Pegasus); there are also sarcophagi, amphorae, everyday utensils, and jewelry.

Today ruins are all that remains of the once magnificent summer residence of Emperor Hadrian, the Villa Adriana.

Tarquinia, Piazza Cavour,
Tel 0766 85 60 36,
Tues–Sun 8.30–19.30.

Villa Adriana The former summer residence of the Emperor Hadrian covers a site of about 120 hectares (296 acres) and contains many reminders of the emperor's extensive travels throughout his empire.
Tivoli, Via Villa Adriana 204,
www.villa-adriana.net,
9.00 until 1 hour before sunset, daily.

Villa d'Este The villa was built for Cardinal Ippolito d'Este between 1550 and 1572. A large-scale Renaissance building in the old medieval city of Tivoli, it is mainly visited for its exquisite garden and water features.
Tivoli, Piazza Trento,
www.villadestetivoli.info,
8.30 until 2 hours before sunset.

FESTIVALS AND EVENTS

Cosmophonies The ancient Roman arena in Ostia Antica forms an atmospheric backdrop for open-air music concerts and performances of drama and dance in the summer.
Tel 06 565 71 49,
www.cosmophonies.com,
June and July.

SPORT, GAMES, FUN

Aquafelix Parco Acquatico A fun and activity water park located near Civitavecchia, north-west of Rome.
www.aquafelix.it

Aquapiper Splash, slide, and swim to your heart's content in this beautifully designed water park close to Guidonia.
www.aquapiper.it

Bagni di Tivoli These thermal baths have been in constant use since ancient times. The "white waters" come from a spring fed by Lago Regina and Lago Colonell. The whiteness of the water is due to the wealth of minerals it contains.
Acque Albule, Via M.
Nicodemi 9, Tivoli,
Tel 0774 354.

Lago di Bolsena Venture out of Rome for the day and visit this beautiful freshwater crater lake where you can swim. It is a 100-km (62-mile) drive via Viterbo, taking the SS 20 to the north-west of Rome. The large lake is located in hilly Latium close to Umbria.
Touristeninformation
Bolsena, Piazza Matteotti,
Tel 0761 77 99 23.

Parco dei Mostri, Bomarzo The "Park of Monsters" is some 90 km (56 miles) north of Rome; the unusual park has impressive, grotesque stone figures in the

From the Capodimonte yachting marina at the Lago di Bolsena you can enjoy superb views of the Castello Farnese.

middle of impenetrable vegetation. Dragons, giant turtles, and fantasy creatures get the imagination going. Plus restaurant and playgrounds.
Tel 0761 92 40 29,
www.parcodeimostri.com,
from 8.00 until sunset, daily.

Castel Fusano Nature Reserve
A nature reserve located near modern Ostia, where you can lie in the sun, swim in the sea, and enjoy the beautiful natural surroundings. The beach is a good 5 km (3 miles) long so there is room for everyone.

Zoomarine Italia, Torvaianica
A large entertainment park for adults and children alike that primarily concentrates on marine animals, but also has a tropical bird forest. There are also activities such as wildwater rafting and other exciting rides for all the family to enjoy.

Tel 06 91 53 40 01,
www.zoomarine.it,
end March to mid-Nov, daily out of season only Sat/Sun.

EATING AND DRINKING

Adriano, Tivoli The restaurant has elegant rooms and a shaded terrace. The cuisine is outstanding and the hotel has played host to many prominent guests, including Queen Elizabeth II, Jacqueline Kennedy, Liv Ullmann, and Federico Fellini. The Hotel Adriano is an ideal place to stay when visiting the Villa Adriana.
Largo Yourcenar 2,
Tel 0774 38 22 35,
www.hoteladriano.it

ACCOMMODATION

Aran Blu Hotel, Lido di Ostia
A modern superior four-star hotel with a steel and glass façade, located opposite the port and very close to the beach, which it overlooks. It also has a private beach for guests. Inside, the Art Caffè is decorated with works by contemporary artists. The hotel benefits from a terrace bar, a restaurant, and a fitness suite.
Lungomare Duca degli
Abruzzi 72,
Tel 06 56 34 02 25,
www.aranhotels.com

Courtyard Rome Airport, Fiumicino Rome With 187 comfortable, modern rooms, this four-star hotel is convenient for visitors arriving in Rome or leaving by plane and in need of overnight accommodation nearby. There is an in-house restaurant, "The Glass", and an outdoor pool that can be used during the summer months.
Via Portuense 2470,
Tel 06 99 93 51,
www.marriott.com

THE ROMAN COUNTRYSIDE AND THE SEA

At the Zoomarine Italia dolphins display their acrobatic skills during popular shows.

Hotel San Marco, Tarquinia This hotel is on the same square as the Museo Nazionale di Tarquinia. The restaurant offers typical regional dishes, some prepared to historical recipes. The American bar stocks over 100 whiskys, rums and cocktails on its list.
Piazza Cavour 18,
Tel 0766 84 22 34,
www.hotelsanmarco.biz

Hotel Relais Castello della Castelluccia The romantic Castello della Castelluccia was built in the 12th and 13th centuries. Situated north-west of Rome and outside the major ring road, this hotel is far removed from the hustle and bustle of the metropolis. It offers a romantic atmosphere and the finest service. Spoil yourself in the restaurant, enjoy the pool and spa facilities, or play a round of golf at the nearby course.

Via Carlo Cavina,
Tel 06 30 20 70 41,
www.lacastelluccia.com

La Posta Vecchia This intimate Renaissance country house is one of the best hotels in the world, according to the trade press. Located right on the coast at Ladispoli, the upscale hotel offers pure luxury and every imaginable service. The 19 rooms and suites are expensively fitted out in keeping with the 17th-century villa – guests are surrounded by valuable antiques. Before it was turned into a luxury hotel, the villa was the home of John Paul Getty, who restored the building at great expense. Hotel guests can visit the in-house museum at any time; but non-residents must apply in advance.
Palo Laziale,
Tel 06 994 95 01,
www.lapostavecchia.com

Residenza D'Epoca Rodrigo de Vivar, Ostia Antica Relax in the country in a cozy, rustic ambience. The hotel's restaurant serves traditional Roman cuisine. In terms of transport, the hotel is conveniently placed: just a few minutes from Fiumicino airport – and when the traffic is quiet, you can be in the heart of Rome in around 30 minutes.
Piazza della Rocca 18.

Villaggio Flaminio Located a good 6 km (4 miles) north of the city, this campsite, which also has small chalets to rent, is a useful alternative to overnight accommodation in city hotels, particularly in terms of cost. There's also a swimming pool to cool you down after some hot city sightseeing.
Via Flaminia Nuova 821,
Tel 06 333 26 04,
all year round, closed in Jan–Feb.

If you want to escape the hustle and bustle of the big city, make sure you visit St. Peter's Square on a normal evening. It's the best way to enjoy the wonderful backdrop surrounding St Peter's Cathedral in peace and quiet.

MAJOR MUSEUMS

Rome is not just extremely rich in monuments, but also boasts a wealth of cultural heritage. When deciding which of the city's museums to visit first, the Vatican Museums are usually top of the list for most visitors, which unfortunately can result in long waits at the entrance. Other outstanding collections include the small but exquisite Galleria Borghese; the national collection of paintings in the Palazzo Barberini; and the Museo Nazionale Romano, one of the largest archeological museums in the world. The Capitoline Museums, the oldest public collection of art and antiques in the world, are particularly noteworthy.

MAJOR MUSEUMS

With more than 50,000 exhibits, the Vatican Museums, comprising a series of individual collections, form the largest self-contained museum complex in the world. The longest of the four tours suggested, guides the visitor around a route of 7 km (over 4 miles). Built up over four centuries by the popes, the museums' collections form a superlative overview of art dating from Antiquity and the Renaissance. The Vatican City lies behind the imposing 15-m (49-ft) high colonnades of St. Peter's Square. The area open to the public includes the museum collections, which are housed in rooms in the former papal palace that were converted to display exhibits as well as in buildings that were constructed expressly as museums. A staircase with an impressive spiral ramp greets the visitor on entering the museum complex; both were designed by the Italian architect Giuseppe Momo (1932).

In addition to the later museum buildings, the Vatican collections are housed in rooms in the papal palace. Most of the building that we see today dates back to the Renaissance popes Nicholas V, Alexander VI, and Julius II. Among the architects employed to work on the palace were Donato Bramante, Baldassare Peruzzi, Giulio Romano, and Jacopo and Andrea Sansovino.

THE HISTORY OF THE COLLECTION

The collection was founded by Pope Julius II (1503–13) with notable ancient pieces such as *Apollo Belvedere*, the *Laocoön* from the Domus Aurea (golden house) of Emperor Nero, the *Antinous Belveder*, and the *Belvedere Torso*.

During German historian Johann Joachim Winckelmann's management of the papal collections (from 1763), additional works of art and other collections were added to the already extensive list of treasures. Many of the rooms in the palace were converted into display areas under Pope Clement XIV (1769–74), and the museum space was further extended during the centuries that followed. The popes were among the first rulers to open their art collections to the public. There are four separate collections: Egyptian, Etruscan, Greco-Roman, and Christian-Western art, with additional rooms with further exhibits in the Vatican palaces. Thanks to a number of donations, there are also several individual museums of note.

EGYPTIAN MUSEUM

Founded under Pope Gregory XVI in 1839, the Museo Gregoriano Egizio exhibits Egyptian antiquities including mummies, sarcophagi, statues, monuments, and rolls of papyrus. Many of the exhibits shown here were originally brought into Italy through trade or as gifts in ancient times, and were found in Rome and its surrounding countryside.

ETRUSCAN MUSEUM

The treasures of the Museo Gregoriano Etrusco offer an insight into the great culture of the Etruscans, the mysterious people who ruled central Italy before the great Roman Empire. The collection includes tombs from the necropolises of Cerveteri, as well as jewelry, bronzes, ceramics, vessels, weapons, tools, and chariots. Among the individual pieces of note are the bronze statue of the so-called Mars of Todi (4th C. BC) and the Stele of Palestrita (5th C. BC).

Left: a view in between the columns of the colonnade opens up an unusual perspective on St Peter's Square.
Below: The Sala Rotonda in the Museo Pio Clementino boasts a fascinating collection of mosaics, sculptures, and busts.

CLASSICAL ANTIQUITIES

The collection of ancient Greek and Roman statues, reliefs, vases, and wall frescoes are principally displayed in the Museo Chiaramonti, the Museo Pio-Clementino, in the Braccio Nuovo, and in the Museo Gregoriano Profano.

In addition to the many portrait busts and statues of emperors and philosophers, the famous works collected by Pope Julius II already mentioned above are worthy of particular attention.

Roman copies of Greek masterpieces such as *Apoxyomenos* (The Scraper) by Lysippus, the *Cnidian Venus* and the *Apollo Sauroktonos* by Praxiteles are impressive – as are the *Doryphoros* (The Spear Bearer) and the *Wounded Amazon* by Polyclitus, the Greek *Three Graces* and the *Athena and Marsyas* by Myron (original, after 450 BC).

MAJOR MUSEUMS

THE SISTINE CHAPEL

Michelangelo Buonarroti, a sculptor and architect, created the ceiling frescoes of the Sistine Chapel on the orders of the pope between 1508 and 1512 – thus proving that he was an ingenious painter too. Since their restoration, the scenes on the ceiling, ranging from the *Creation of the World* to the *Drunkenness of Noah*, are vibrant and vivid. The scenes form an incredibly complicated system of painted architecture and painted sculptures, in front of which have been placed the figures of prophets, sibyls, and naked boys. Michelangelo thus surpassed the previous art of ceiling painting in which the

---

Original Roman works of note include the statue of *Augustus* of Primaporta and the fresco of the *Aldobrandini Wedding*.

CHRISTIAN-WESTERN ART

The Museo Pio Cristiano and the Vatican library, designed by Domenico Fontana in 1587, exhibit a collection of relics, liturgical objects, and small precious items made from materials such as ivory, glass, metal, and textiles, many dating back to the early Christian period. The inspiring and beautiful *Perseus with the Head of Medusa*, a masterpiece of classicism by Antonio Canova (1800), is on display in the Cortile del Belvedere.

VATICAN PALACES

The Appartamento Borgia of Pope Alexander VI contains six rooms decorated with fine frescoes by Pinturicchio and artists from his studio between 1492 and 1495; modern religious art is also on display here. The superb loggias and the three Stanze di Raffaeollo ("Raphael's rooms") are especially worth making the extra effort to visit.

The latter, dating from the early 16th century, represent one of the pinnacles of Renaissance painting: the Stanza della Segnatura contains one of the best-known works by Raphael, *The School of Athens*, which depicts philosophers and scientists from ancient times, and the *Disputà del Sacramento* portraying images of the saints; the other stanze include the beautiful frescoes *Fire in the Borgo* and the *Expulsion of Heliodorus from the Temple*. The chapel of Pope Nicholas V was decorated in around 1455 by Fra Angelico with scenes from the lives of St Laurence and St Stephen. The Sistine Chapel (see above), constructed between 1473 and 1484, however, is home to Michelangelo's world-famous masterpiece, including the ceiling frescoes with scenes from the story of the creation in eight individual scenes, including one of the best-known images in the art world, *The Creation of Adam,* as well as the *Last Judgment* on the altar wall, which he painted between 1534 and 1541, almost three decades after the ceiling painting.

PINACOTECA VATICANA

The paintings in the collection of the Pinacoteca Vaticana are arranged chronologically in a building constructed specifically for displaying the valuable works of art in 1932. Among its main attractions include the wall tapestries designed by

images were set inside smaller fields of stucco or wood. From 1980 the Sistine Chapel and its frescoes were lavishly restored and ceremoniously re-inaugurated in late 1999.

A breathtakingly beautiful sight: Michelangelo's ceiling in the Sistine Chapel.

Raphael originally for the Sistine Chapel, the *Madonna of Foligno*, and the *Transfiguration of Christ* created by the same artist.

Giotto's *Stefaneschi Triptych* is impressive, as is the *Deposition from the Cross* by Caravaggio; there are also very fine pieces by other major Italian artists including Leonardo da Vinci, Bellini, Titian, Paolo Veronese, Guido Reni, Murillo, and Jose de Ribera, among others.

Vatican Museums,
Viale Vaticano,
Tel 06 69 88 49 47,
April–Oct. Mon–Sat
8.45–16.45 Uhr, Nov–March
8.45–13.45,
Underground: Cipro-Musei
Vaticani.

Left: Guido Reni painted his *Crucifixion of St. Peter* in 1604; Pinacoteca.

MAJOR MUSEUMS

Relatively small in size, the Galleria Borghese and its collection of sculptures and paintings make it one of Rome's best museums. In its overall shape it still conveys the fact that it began life as a private collection, whose holdings of ancient as well as more recent art treasures reflect the passi-on the dukes had for collecting and for displaying their posses-sions. The so-called Casino Borghese, the actual villa with its beautiful exterior and impo-sing flight of stairs, features marble decorations and fresco-es inside, for example, *Camillus after the parley with Brennus, commander of the Gallic army* and *Allegory of Time* by Maria-no Rossi. Built expressly as a gallery for the display of works of art, the building is not mere-ly functional structure but in-stead a work of art in itself. The English style Villa Borghese Gardens are also a popular tourist attraction and a work of art in themselves.

The Villa Borghese was desig-ned by architects Giovanni Vasanzio and Flaminio Ponzio for Cardinal Scipio Borghese, from the noble House of Borg-hese, who had acquired the land on which it was to be built – located in the vineyards – in 1605. The cardinal then had the surrounding area con-verted into a formal and geo-metrically ordered park and garden. The layout of the cur-rent park dates from the 18th century, when it was converted to the English style in keeping with the tastes of the time. When the weather is fine, visi-tors can fly over the property in hot-air balloons (mongolfieres) and enjoy all the surroundings from above.

THE HISTORY
OF THE COLLECTION

Scipio Caffarelli Borghese's magnificent villa on the Pincio Hill beyond the city walls was constructed between 1613 and 1616, as a place in which he could present his superb col-lection of ancient sculptures. The stunning interio today is mostly thanks to a redesign car-ried out in the mid-18th century. In 1807, Camillo Borghese, who was married to Napoleon Bonaparte's sister Paolina, was pressurized by the French em-peror to sell the Borghese col-lection to France and conse-quently this part of the collection can today be seen in the Louvre in Paris.

However, the Borghese family went on to acquire further an-cient sculptures, which were also displayed at the villa. In 1891 the family's valuable col-lection of paintings was added, which until then had been kept in the family's palace in Rome. In 1902, the villa complex pas-sed to the Italian state and the park to the municipality.

GROUND FLOOR

The rooms on the ground floor primarily contain sculptures along with some Roman floor mosaics dating from the AD 3rd century and some paintings, including works by Annibale Carracci and Guido Reni. Parti-cularly outstanding sculptural works are the statue of Empe-ror Augustus in his role as supreme priest and a Roman copy of Athena Parthenos. The original of the latter, now lost, was made of gold and ivory and stood approximately 12 m (39 ft) in height. A religious effigy of the goddess Athena, it was created around 440 BC for the Parthenon on the Acropolis in Athens by the Greek sculptor Phidias.

Among other highlights of the Galleria Borghese are figures by Giovanni Lorenzo Bernini, commissioned by Scipio Borg-hese especially for his art

Left: the magnificent main entrance to the Casino Borghese featuring a richly ornamented façade.
Below: Paolina Borghese, Napoleon's sister, depicted as Venus, by Antonio Canova, 1805–1808.

MAJOR MUSEUMS

APOLLO AND DAPHNE

The life-size pairing of *Apollo and Daphne*, one of the key works created by the sculptor and architect Gianlorenzo Bernini between 1622– and 1625, portrays an episode from Ovid's *Metamorphoses*. According to a legend from ancient Greek mythology, retold throughout history, the story goes that the god Apollo desired the nymph Daphne. However, she did not return his love and took flight. Apollo tried to catch her, but as he reached her she slipped away forever, turning into a laurel tree (*daphne* in Greek) to escape him, her arms becoming branches, her skin bark and her

collection between 1620 and 1625. These are some of the celebrated baroque sculptor and architect's early works and include Apollo and Daphne, *Pluto and Proserpina*, the statue of a youthful David, as well as *Aeneas, Anchises and Ascanius Fleeing Troy.*

Further works by Bernini, including the *Personification of Truth*, produced around 1655, were later additions to the collection. However, all these works show his masterly handling of marble, his wonderful use of light and shade, and the emotion that he brought to his work, so characteristic of the baroque period.

Bernini often chose to focus on pivotal moments in history, such as depicting a youthful David during his altercations with Goliath in the act of hurling his stone at him. Full of life and movement, his work can be contrasted with the re-strained and fairly cool classicism of Antonio Canova's masterpiece *Paolina Borghese* (1805–1808), in which Canova depicts Napoleon's sister as Venus reclining on a couch. The sculpting of the folds of the fabric is particularly fine.

UPPER FLOOR

This part of the gallery is mainly devoted to the display of the valuable painting collection, which primarily dates from the Italian Renaissance and the baroque period. Also exhibited here are busts by Bernini, including two portraying his client Scipio Borghese, and his bozzetto (clay model) for an "equestrian statue of King Louis XIV of France", as well as ancient and baroque sculptures by other artists.

For examples of outstanding Renaissance art, look for pieces by Antonello da Messina, Giovanni Bellini, Lorenzo Lotto, and Paolo Veronese, and particularly Raphael's famous *Deposition*, or *The Entombment*, as well as two portraits by Raphael: the mysterious *Young Woman with Unicorn* (c. 1506) and the *Portrait of a Man* featuring chubby cheeks (c. 1502). Also impressive are Correggio's *Danae* (c. 1531), depicting an episode from Ovid's *Metamorphoses*, and Titian's masterly *Sacred and Profane Love* (c. 1514).

A good example of the mannerist style is Agnolo Bronzino's *John the Baptist* (c. 1525).

Caravaggio's paintings are fine examples of early Roman baroque, including the *Madonna dei Palafrenieri* with Mary, the infant Jesus, and Anna, Mary's mother; the *Sick Bacchus*, a self-portrait of the artist; and *St. Jerome.*

Works by Domenichino, Pietro da Cortona, the German Lucas

toes turning to roots. However she remained eternally linked with the god of the arts as a symbol of glory.

Bernini succeeded in producing a remarkably lifelike, dramatic sculpture, in which skin, hair, leaves, and roots are all beautifully reproduced in cold, unforgiving marble, thus retelling this great story. Engraved on the cartouche on the base are the words: *Those who love to pursue fleeting forms of pleasure, in the end find only leaves and bitter berries in their hands.*

Apollo and Daphne (1622–1625) by Gianlorenzo Bernini.

Cranach the Elder, and the Flemish baroque artist Peter Paul Rubens are also particularly impressive.

Venus and Cupid with a Honeycomb painted by the Renaissance artist, Cranach in around 1531, is a fine example of this Flemish-trained artist's work.

Pieter Paul Rubens, the genius of European Baroque, painted his *Deposition* during his first stay in Rome; it explores the incarnation of the divine and human nature of Christ

Galleria Borghese, Piazzale del Museo Borghese 5 Tel 06 84 13 979, Tues–Sun 8.30–19.00, tickets: Tel 06 328 10 or www.ticketeria.it

Left top: *Sick Bacchus* by **Caravaggio (1594);**
Below: *The Deposition* by the **masterly Raphael (1507).**

MAJOR MUSEUMS

The National Gallery of Ancient Art's collection of paintings housed in the former city palace of the Barberini family contains an impressive cross section of European paintings from the Middle Ages onward. A significant number of the exhibits once belonged to noble Roman families. The Palazzo Corsini shows the significant paintings of the Galleria Corsini. An associated collection of graphic art is located in the Villa Farnesina. The Palazzo Barberini is a perfect example of a grand Roman house of the baroque period, and its size is equally impressive. Laid out around three sides of a fore- court, with wide arched windows and hardly any wall area between them, the building is typical of its period. The rich ornamentation and frescoes inside are also highly characteristic. Palazzo Barberini set a style, and the features used in the palace of northern Italy were now adopted in Rome.

The most important baroque city palace in Rome was commissioned by Maffeo Barberini for the Baberini family – he later became Pope Urban VIII – and was designed by architects Carlo Maderno, Gianlorenzo Bernini, and Francesco Borromini. Worthy of particular attention are its two staircases: on the right, a spiral staircase in oval form by Borromini; and on the left, a rectangular staircase by Bernini. In the Gran Salone, located on the second floor, the ceiling fresco by Pietro da Cortona glorifies the Barberini dynasty. The three bees are their heraldic symbol. Other frescoes were painted by Andrea Sacchi.

The Palazzo Corsini (1729–1732), situated on the western side of the Tiber, can be traced back in its present form to Fernando Fuga. The Villa Farnesina (1508–1511) nearby is the work of Baldassare Peruzzi; its interior contains frescoes by Raphael, Giulio Romano, Baldassare Peruzzi himself, Sebastiano del Piombo, and Sodoma.

PALAZZO BARBERINI

The works in the collection housed in the Palazzo Barberini are displayed in chronological order, with the first floor being mainly devoted to Italian paintings from the 12th to 17th centuries, along with Flemish, French, and German paintings as well. These include such masterpieces as Raphael's portrait of *La Fornarina*. The features of the unknown sitter, who also appears in other works by Raphael, have – at least since the Romantic period – been believed to be that of the artist's great love and inspirational muse. Other highlights of the museum include Titian's *Venus and Adonis*, several Passion scenes by Tintoretto, as well as his Christ and the *Woman Taken in Adultery*, Caravaggio's *Judith and Holofernes* and *Narcissus* by the same artist. The collection includes works by Renaissance artists such as Filippo Lippi, Lorenzo Lotto, and Sodoma, and mannerist painters such as Agnolo Bronzino and El Greco. Another part of the collection features Roman, Neapolitan, and Bolognese baroque painting, with work by Pietro da Cortona, Giovanni Lanfranco, Luca Giordano, Mattia Preti, Guercino, Domenichino, and Guido Reni. In the Palazzo Barberini you can also see a *Portrait of King Henry VIII of England*, by court painter Hans Holbein the Younger, and the well-known Portrait of Erasmus of Rotterdam by Quentin Massys.

The second floor of the Palazzo Barberini is filled with paintings from the 18th century,

GALLERIA NAZIONALE D'ARTE ANTICA

Left: the main façade of the Galleria Nazionale d'Arte Antica.
Below: *The Massacre of the Niobids*, a mythological scene by Andrea Camassei, 1640.

MAJOR MUSEUMS

AN OLD TESTAMENT STORY GETS A DRAMATIC TWIST

Michelangelo Merisi da Caravaggio's depiction of the biblical scene of Judith and Holofernes shows Judith, who became a heroine for the people of Israel when she freed her native town of Bethulia from the Assyrians. The town was besieged and had almost run out of fresh water, when Judith, a widow, crept out and made her way into the Assyrians' camp and the tent of the enemy commander Holofernes.

She seduced him with alchohol and promised that he would be able to capture Bethulia, but after a feast, she cut off the drunken commander's

primarily of Italian and French origin, as well as works made by artisans, including Rome vedutas (large-scale city views) by Vanvitelli and Venice vedutas by Canaletto. The original Appartamento Settecentesco of Cornelia Costanza Barberini, furnished between 1750 and 1770, offers a glimpse into the aristocratic life of the times, and contains furniture, porcelain, and jewelry.

PALAZZO CORSINI

The Palazzo Corsini mainly displays works from the Corsini family collection, which was sold to the Italian state in 1883 along with the palace itself. The collection was begun by the avid collector Cardinal Neri Maria Corsini. The palace still has associations with Queen Christina of Sweden, who had abdicated, moved to Rome and lived in an earlier palace on the site from 1659 until her death in 1689.

The exhibits are mostly Italian paintings from the 14th to the 17th century are arranged by landscapes and also encompass religious and historical works. They include pieces by Fra Angelico, Annibale Carracci, Luca Giordano, Giovanni Lanfranco, Guido Reni, Carlo Maratta, and successors to Caravaggio such as Orazio Gentileschi – and also pieces by Peter Paul Rubens, Anthony van Dyck, Esteban Murillo, Jose de Ribera, and Angelica Kauffmann. Finally, the Palazzo is also the seat of the Accademia Nazionale dei Lincei, which was founded in 1603, closed in 1630 and refounded in 1847 as Pontifical Academy of New Lincei. This academy of the sciences also once counted Galileo Galilei among its members. The academy has some rare and valuable works of art.

GABINETTO NAZIONALE DELLE STAMPE

The national graphic art collection is housed in the Villa Farnesina and has more than 150,000 drawings and prints from the 15th to the 19th century. Built for a rich banker and the treasurer of Pope Julius II at the beginning of the 16th century, it was intended as a summer retreat. Acquired by the Farnese family in 1577, it is now owned by the state.

Palazzo Barberini,
Via delle Quattro Fontane 13,
Palazzo Corsini, Via della
Lungara 10, Villa Farnesina,
Via della Lungara 230,
Tel 06 48 45 91.

Right top: *Victorian family in the Garden* by C. J. Langley, 1850; **Below:** *Saint John Francis Regis* by Domenico Muratori, 1740.

GALLERIA NAZIONALE D'ARTE ANTICA

head. Caravaggio portrays the full brutality of the act of murder in his painting. in which the servant holds the bag as Judith wields the knife. Famed for his realism and sense of drama, Caravaggio made use of light and dark to highlight the essential part of a painting to which he wanted to draw the viewer's attention, while concealing everything else from view. The painter of the early Baroque perfectly manages to dramatize the story by showing the exact moment of its climax.

Judith and Holofernes by Caravaggio, 1598.

MAJOR MUSEUMS

The Museo Nazionale Romano (the National Museum of Rome) is one of the largest and most important archeological museums in the world. Due to the immense size of the collection, it is displayed in three different building complexes in separate locations, with only two of them however in close vicinity to each other – the Terme di Diocleziano (the Baths of Diocletian), and the Palazzo Massimo – whereas the third building, the Palazzo Altemps built in 1480 is located some way further west, near the Piazza Navona.

Built in the 19th century, the Museo alle Terme was formerly a Jesuit seminary, and was used as a military hospital in World War II. Acquired by the state in 1981, it was restored and adapted to house part of the museum's collection. It exhibits many superb ancient sculptures, including the relief of a gladiatorial battle dating from the 2nd century.

Founded in 1889, the National Museum of Rome was initially housed in an abandoned 16th-century Carthusian monastery, which had been built over the remains of the baths of Emperor Diocletian, the largest of all the imperial Roman baths. Today, the museum still contains many sculptures, objects from everyday life in ancient Rome, and a collection of inscriptions. IThe Aula Ottagona (Octagonal Hall), which is also part of the baths complex, displays some of the sculpture collection, along with a collection of inscriptions and stele (funeral stones). The Palazzo Massimo, not far away, is home to the principal sculpture collection, and also contains a coin collection and frescoes. The Palazzo Altemps meanwhile, located nearby north of Piazza Navona, houses the exceptionally important Ludovisi and Mattei collections.

TERME DI DIOCLEZIANO

Visitors walk through a garden containing tomb stelae, stone sarcophagi, and relief fragments to gain access to the main part of the museum, which has on display archeological finds from the pre- and early history of Rome (10th to 7th centuries BC. In the former thermae, the museum's first location, Roman architectural fragments, statues, sarcophagi, and mosaics Sare exhibited as well as items of everyday use and weapons, all excavated at sites in around Rome.

In the Aula Ottagona, one of the largest domed rooms in the baths with its own entrance, two statues stand out among the many figures on display (most of which are Roman copies of Greek masterpieces): *The Athlete* and *The Boxer*. These two bronze sculptures from the Hellenistic period are superbly sculpted with great realism – the boxer's scars and broken nose are visible. The epigraphical collection containing numerous inscriptions is also shown in this part of the museum.

PALAZZO MASSIMO

Built at the end of the 19th century, the Palazzo Massimo was once part of a Jesuit college. The exhibits on display represent the various themes and styles prevalent in ancient Rome between the 2nd and 4th centuries until the end of the imperial period, discovered in various locations in and around the city. Mosaics and sculptures are displayed on the ground floor, including many busts and statues of Roman emperors. The Emperor Augustus is depicted as Pontifex Maximus (supreme priest) with a toga drawn up over his head.

MUSEO NAZIONALE ROMANO

Top: The Palazzo Massimo, which was built for the Jesuit Massimiliano Massimo between 1883 and 1887.
Middle: Gladiatiors, fighting around AD 100.
Bottom: A relic from a glorious past. Roman marbles sarcophagus with relief, dating from around AD 100.

HERMES LUDOVISI

This marble statue of Hermes, the messenger of the gods, easily recognizable by his winged helmet, is a Roman 1st-century copy of a Greek bronze original from around 440 BC attributed to Phidias. After Hellas (the ancient Greek name for Greece) was incorporated into the Roman Empire, Greek works of art were very much in vogue and were so coveted by the Romans that they had many statues brought to Rome from Greece. In order to meet the enormous demand from wealthy private clients and for public statues, many pieces were copied in considerable numbers. The copies were usu-

Also located on the ground floor is the famous *Wounded Niobid*, a figure depicting the daughter of Queen Niobe of Thebes attempting to pull out the arrow which was shot by Apollo. This copy of a classical Greek original from about 440 BC was initially believed to have been produced for a temple pediment.

The valuable coin collection of the Italian royal family and a collection of ancient jewelry are also displayed in the Palazzo Massimo.

On the first floor, in addition to sarcophagi and busts of the emperors, Roman copies of famous Greek sculptures predominate: there are two copies of *The Discus Thrower* by Myron (around 450 BC; the *Anzio Apollo* after Praxiteles (late 4th century BC); and *Crouching Aphrodite* after Doidalsas (3rd century BC). The second floor displays Roman frescoes – including frescoes from the dining room of Livia Drusilla's villa, the wife of Emperor Augustus, depicting a garden landscape complete with fruit and birds. This can only be seen as part of a guided tour.

PALAZZO ALTEMPS

In recent years, the important Ludovisi and Mattei collections have been re-housed in the former city palace of Cardinal Markus Sittikus von Hohenem (Altemps), which also reflects the passion for collection and the ideals of the 16th century. Begun in 1477, the palace building was expanded in the 16th century by several major Renaissance architects, including Antonio da Sangallo the Elder, Baldassare Peruzzi, and Martino Longhi.

Particularly outstanding exhibits in the collection are the *Hermes Ludovisi* (a Hellenistic sculpture of the god Hermes) and the head of Juno Ludovisi (a colossal head of the goddess Juno), which was particularly highly prized in the 18th century. A counterpart to the sculpture of the *Dying Gaul* in the Palazzo Nuovo on the Capitoline Hill is the group *Gaul Killing Himself and his Wife*. The Ludovisi Battle Sarcophagus is a Roman work from the 3rd century AD depicting the conquering of barbarians by the Romans.

But perhaps the best-known piece in the collection is the *Trono Ludovisi* (The Ludovisi Throne), which is not really a throne but a block of marble with a hollowed back and a relief showing Aphrodite rising from the sea. It is thought by some experts to be a Greek original, but a modern forgery by others.

In addition to the classical treasures in the Palazzo

MUSEO NAZIONALE ROMANO

ally created in marble rather than bronze. Many of the originals no longer exist, having been melted down for scrap, mainly it is believed, in the Middle Ages.

So it is thanks to these ancient Roman copies that we still have knowledge of the Greek masterpieces today. No single original work of Phidias exists today, but copies, cameos, coins and numerous written reports attest to his genius and mastery of his art.

Hermes Ludovisi, Roman marble copy of a bronze original by the Greek sculptor Phidias (5th century BC).

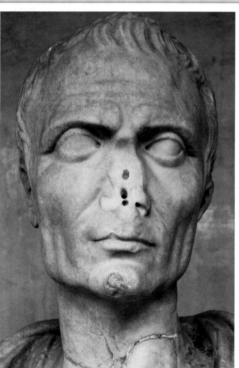

Altemps, there several important Egyptian pieces now displayed in rooms recently opened to the public for the first time. The statue of the black bull-deity Apis, from the Brancaccio collection, dominates the Sala dei culti pubblici e privati, and the space and lighting allows the visitor to appreciate the magnificence of the black diorite bull. Apis was worshipped in Egypt's ancient capital Memphis and during Roman times was associated with the cult of Isis.

Museo Nazionale Romano:
Terme di Diocleziano mit
Aula Ottagona, Palazzo
Massimo alle Terme,
Palazzo Altemps,
Tel 06 39 96 77 00,
Tues–Sun 9.00–19.45.

Left: statesman and general – a marble portrait of Gaius Julius Caesar, 1st century. BC

MAJOR MUSEUMS

The large collections of the Capitoline Museums are mainly housed in three palaces on the Capitoline Hill – the Palazzo Nuovo and the Palazzo dei Conservatori, on the Piazza del Campidoglio, and the adjacent Palazzo Caffarelli-Clementino. Considered the oldest public collection of art and antiquities in the world, because the starting point of the collection was gifted to the people of Rome by Pope Clement XI and the collection was first opened to the public in 1734 when it was housed in the Palazzo Nuovo. When the Palazzo Nuovo was built in 1650, it was styled on the Renaissance Palazzo dei Conservatori on the opposite side of the Piazza del Campidoglio to unify the architecture. The gilded bronze original of the Marcus Aurelius equestrian statue (2nd century BC) stands in the Palazzo dei Conservatori, where the arm from a statue of Emperor Constantine is also on display.

The Palazzo Nuovo, situated on the Piazza del Campidoglio, is the original site and main location of the collection. It was built in 1650, reflecting the Renaissance style of the Palazzo dei Conservatori opposite. The Palazzo dei Conservatori was built between 1564 and 1575 by Guido Guidetti and Giacomo della Porta to plans by Michelangelo, on whose plans the design of the whole square is based.

THE HISTORY OF THE COLLECTION

In 1471, Pope Sixtus IV donated a group of important ancient bronzes to the city of Rome, which were to form the basis of the museum collection. The statues had previously been held in the former papal residence, the Lateran Palace. They included the *Capitoline Wolf*, *Spinario* (a boy removing a thorn from his foot), the figure known as *Camillus*, as well as the head and two fragments of a colossal statue of the Emperor Constantine. The collection was moved to the Capitoline Hill, the ancient religious and present-day political heart of Rome. The collection was steadily expanded by finds from excavations, and in 1653 it was installed in the Palazzo Nuovo.

In 1734, after the purchase of the Albani Collection, the Palazzo Nuovo was converted into a museum and opened to the public – a development that was unusual for the times. In 1749, another collection of paintings was added through a donation made by Pope Benedict XIV. Following the unification of Italy, in 1870 the museum passed into state ownership. It was expanded in 1876, through the inclusion of the Palazzo dei Conservatori and the adjacent Palazzo Caffarelli-Clementino, along with the remains of other ancient buildings on the Capitoline.

PALAZZO NUOVO

The remains of temples dedicated to the Capitoline Triad – the three Roman supreme deities (Jupiter, Juno, and Minerva) – are displayed in the basement of the Palazzo Nuovo, together with part of the Tabularium, the building that contained ancient Rome's state archive, while the ground floor and first floor are devoted to sculptural exhibits. In addition to busts of Roman emperors and philosophers, look out for *The Drunken Old Woman*, a rather grotesque but realistic sculpture of an old woman clutching a pitcher of wine, typical of the Hellenistic period, and *The Capitoline Venus*, a Roman copy of a Greek

CAPITOLINE MUSEUMS

Left: a copy of the equestrian statue of Emperor Marcus Aurelius stands in front of the Palazzo dei Conservatori .
Below: one of the greatest treasures in the Pinacoteca Capitolina is *Romulus and Remus* by Peter Paul Rubens, 1614.

MAJOR MUSEUMS

THE CAPITOLINE WÖLF

This bronze sculpture of the famous symbol of the city of Rome – the she-wolf suckling Romulus and Remus, now in the Palazzo dei Conservatori – was originally thought to date from the Etruscan period, and the figures of the twins to have been added in the late 15th century, possibly by the Renaissance sculptor Antonio del Pollaiuolo. However, according to recent research by experts into casting techniques and radiocarbon dating, the whole sculpture is now thought to be from the Middle Ages, probably the 13th century. It has also been suggested that it was commissioned to

masterpiece by Praxiteles (4th century BC. Two copies of a *Wounded Amazon*, one after Polyclitus, the other after Phidias – the originals were said to have been created in a competition between the two artists to see who could produce the best sculpture – are also highlights of this collection. The *Dying Gaul* is another Roman copy of a figure from the Greek city of Pergamum in modern-day Turkey, celebrating the victory of the Pergamese over the Gauls. It depicts the dying Celt with touching realism.

PALAZZO DEI CONSERVATORI

The remains of a colossal marble statue of the Emperor Constantine can be seen in the courtyard of the Palazzo dei Conservatori. Exhibits on the first floor include The Capitoli-

ne Wolf, Spinario, Camillus, and the remains of a bronze statue of Constantine, as well as Brutus, a strikingly realistic bronze bust (look at the eyes) and a masterpiece of Etruscan-Roman art of the 2nd century BC. The Sala Marco Aurelio, the new glass-covered hall now contains the bronze (originally gold-plated) equestrian statue of Emperor Marcus Aurelius (emperor AD 161–180). In the Middle Ages, it was thought to be of the Christian Emperor Constantine and therefore escaped being melted down. In 1538, when the Capitoline was redesigned, the statue was moved from its old location in front of the Lateran Palace to the Capitoline Hill and stood in the middle of the Piazza del Campidoglio until the 1980s. After restoration, and in order to preserve it, the statue in the piazza was replaced by a copy and the original placed in the

Sala Marco Aurelio, a new glass-covered hall. The emperor is shown mounted on a horse, one hand outstretched in a commanding but relaxed pose. It became the model for many equestrian statues.

The second floor displays collections of coins, ancient stone carvings, and jewelry.

PINACOTECA CAPITOLINA

The Pinacoteca Capitolina is the Capitoline Museums' collection of paintings, also housed on the second floor of the Palazzo dei Conservatori. Dating mainly from the Renaissance period and the Roman and Bolognese baroque, it includes works by Veronese, Tintoretto, the *Baptism of Christ* by a young Titian, *The Fortune Teller* and *John the Baptist* by Caravaggio, *Romulus and Remus Suckled by the She-Wolf* by Rubens, the *Cumaean Sibyl*

replace an ancient statue that had been destroyed. However, other investigations have indicated that the material structure of the bronze is typical of that of ancient times and not the Middle Ages.

Left: There is speculation about the age of the *Capitoline Wolf*.

and the *Persian Sibyl* by Guercino, some important later works by Guido Reni, and The *Rape of the Sabines* by Pietro da Cortona.

MUSEO MONTEMARTINI

Further exhibits from the Capitoline Museum collection are displayed at the Museo Montemartini in a modern, industrial setting in a former electricity power plant in the south of Rome. Among the highlights are the remains of the figures in the temple of Apollo Sosiano.

Kapitolinische Museen, Piazza del Campidoglio 1, Museo Montemartini, Viale Ostiense 106, Tel 06 82 05 91 27, Tues-Sun 9.00–20.00, bus 95, 117, 119, 160, 175, 850.

Esquiline Venus – a Greek statue in the Palazzo dei Conservatori.

The Vatican forms an enclave on the western banks of the River Tiber in Rome. The colonnades created by Bernini line St Peter's Square, which is adorned by an Egyptian obelisk.

Few visitors can resist the charm of Rome with its bustling maze of alleys and stairways, piazzas and colonnades, markets, shops, and cafés, all bathed in a magical golden light on a warm Roman evening. To the tourist, the monuments that stand on almost every street corner, some of them thousands of years old, may seem like a decorative detail. On these strolls through the city you can fully take in the Roman way of life, while experiencing all the different things that each individual district has to offer and at the same time go on a journey back in time to the fascinating history of the Eternal City.

The Colosseum features three floors on top of each other, with arcades forming the fourth and final floor.

SIGHTS

❶ The Colosseum Built in AD 72–80 the Colosseum's name is believed to derive from a colossal statue of the emperor Nero situated nearby. An arena for the staging of gladiatorial battles and the baiting of animals, it seated some 75,000 spectators, had an awning that sheltered the spectators from the sun, and a well-planned system of entrances and exits.

❷ The Arch of Constantine Constantine's triumphal arch was erected by the Roman senate in AD 312–315 following the emperor's victory over his rival Maxentius at the Battle of Milvian Bridge. The arch is one of the best-preserved ancient monuments in Rome.

❸ The Arch of Titus The oldest remaining triumphal arch in Rome stands at the entrance to the Forum Romanum. It is a memorial to the conquest of Jerusalem in AD 70 by Titus, who later became emperor. The arch has an impressive, balanced, classical shape; the reliefs on the inside of the arch are famous, showing Titus' triumphant return with the loot from the temple at Jerusalem, including the seven-branched candelabra, the menorah.

❹ Forum Romanum The Roman Forum was the public heart of the ancient city and the political focal point of the empire. Temples and state buildings, such as the Curia – the meeting place of the Roman Senate – were complemented by triumphal arches, rostrums, halls for legal and business affairs, market stalls, and taverns.

❺ Trajan's Column The Imperial Forums adjoin the Roman Forum and are today cut through by the Via dei Fori Imperiali constructed under Mussolini. Trajan's Column, erected in AD 110–113 in Trajan's Forum, once had a gold-plated statue of the emperor on top (now replaced by St Peter), and held the ashes of

Trajan in an urn in its base. The spiral reliefs narrate the story of the emperor's glorious campaigns against the Dacians.

⑥ Santa Maria in Aracoeli
In medieval times, this was the political heart of Rome, where the city council met. The Franciscan church, located at the top of a steep flight of steps, is worth the strenuous ascent for its numerous tombs and a fresco by Pinturicchio (around 1485). At Christmas time, children say prayers and read sermons before the Santo Bambino, a miraculous statue of the infant Jesus.

⑦ The Capitol The religious heart of ancient Rome – the temple of Jupiter Optimus Maximus (the king of the gods)

The Marcellus Theater was commissioned by Emperor Augustus.

was located here – is today topped by a square designed by Michelangelo. On opposite sides of the square, the Palazzo Nuovo and the Palazzo dei Conservatori are home to the Capitoline Museums. The well-known equestrian statue of Emperor Marcus Aurelius in the middle is a copy.

8 Teatro di Marcello The oldest surviving Roman theater, on which a Renaissance palace was later built, is a venue today for concerts in the summer months.

9 Forum Boarium In the cattle market of the ancient city and its adjacent vegetable market (Forum Holitorium) are two well-preserved Roman temples, the rectangular temple of Portunus, god of ports, and a round building known as the Temple of Vesta, which was actually dedicated to Hercules.

10 Santa Maria in Cosmedin This church was built in the 8th century on the remains of an ancient temple. The 12th-century Cosmatesque work (inlaid ornamental mosaics) is particularly fine. In the portico, the Bocca della Verità, the Mouth of Truth, an old drain cover, is supposed believed to clamp shut on the hand of anyone who lies.

11 Santa Sabina In ancient times the Aventine Hill was densely populated, but today it is a more tranquil spot. The early Christian church of Santa Sabina, dating from the 5th century, is known for its cedarwood door, featuring biblical scenes, and its interior decorated with marble. At the far end of the Via di Santa Sabina is the Piazza dei Cavalieri di Malta, with the priory of the Order of the Knights of Malta. If you look through the keyhole in the

garden gate, you'll see the famous view of the dome of St Peter's Basilica.

SHOPPING

1 Gusto Italia di Angelo Biagi A tempting shop, located not far from the Coliseum, specializing in gourmet products from a number of small Italian family businesses in the region (making wines, pasta, cheese, pastries, etc.). Good prices and outstanding quality.
Via Leonina 76,
Tel 06 47 82 37 00,
www.gustoitalia.it

2 Le Gallinelle Fashion designer Wilma Silvestri knows how to get the best out of all different fabrics – some from Asia, some recycled – and transforms them into wonderful, bold clothes, sold at reasonable prices. Visitors to Rome with enough time can commis-

Some ancient stones were reused to build the church of Santa Maria in Cosmedin.

sion outfits made to measure. Silvestri's collections are also presented in fashion shows.
Via dei Serpenti 27,
www.legallinelle.it

3 Leone Limentani In the heart of the former ghetto, this family-run tableware and kitchen equipment company has been trading for seven generations. It stocks classic styles and novel designs, and many of the items make great gifts. Make sure you don't get lost in this fascinating shop's many passageways and rooms.
Via del Portico d' Ottavia 47,
Tel 06 68 80 66 86,
www.limentani.com

4 Flea market in the Piazza Porta Portese The largest flea market in Rome takes place in this square every Sunday – it's also one of the largest and liveliest in Europe. Arrive early to avoid the worst of the crush, and keep a sharp eye out for counterfeit products, overpriced items, and pickpockets!
Piazza di Porta Portese and
its side streets,
Sunday from 5.00.

EATING AND DRINKING

5 Alle Carrette A rustic pizzeria not far from the Imperial Forums, but the entrance is not easy to find. The pizzas and salads are really wonderful.
Via della Madonna dei Monti
95, Tel 06 679 27 70,
Tues–Sun evenings.

6 Baires If you are hankering after a good steak, head for this Argentinean restaurant. The portions are generous and the food delicious.
Via Cavour 315,
Tel 06 69 20 21 64,
www.baires.it,
Mon–Sun 12.00–24.00.

7 Giggetto al Portico d'Ottavia Roman Jewish cuisine is simple but tasty, relatively uninfluenced by current trends, and is better here than almost anywhere else in the city. Claudio Ceccarelli buys his ingredients fresh every morning. Try the artichokes and the baccalà (dried cod), the house specials.
Via del Portico d'Ottavia
21 a/22, Tel 06 686 11 05,
www.giggetto.it,
Tues–Sun 12.30–15.00,
19.30–23.00.

8 Sora Lella This trattoria on the Isola Tiberina is a real institution and has been in the same family for over 65 years. The dishes are typically Roman cuisine with lavish, delicious portions.
Via di Ponte Quattro Capi 16,
Tel 06 686 16 01,
www.soralella.com,
Mon–Sat 12.45–14.30,
19.30–22.30.

One of the main attractions in the city on the Tiber are the Spanish Steps, a popular meeting point day and night.

SIGHTS

 Piazza del Popolo In former times, people arriving from the north would enter the city here. The church of Santa Maria del Popolo near the city gate is a little gem of art history, with works by Caravaggio, Annibale Carracci, Pinturicchio, Raphael, and Bernini.

❷ The Spanish Steps Over the Pincio Hill with its beautiful view of Rome, past the Villa Medici and the French Academy and the church of Santa Trinità dei Monti, you'll end up at the most impressive and famous steps in the whole of Rome – the Spanish Steps (1723–1726) with their glorious organic curves. The Piazza di Spagna below was once an artists' quarter. Today, it is where the sophisticated shopping streets around the Via Condotti converge.

❸ Propaganda Fide The Palazzo di Propaganda Fide, the missionary headquarters of the Catholic Church, belongs to the Vatican City. The façade on the side facing the square was created by Giovanni Bernini, while the façade with the turned pillars on the Via Propaganda was created by his rival Francesco Borromini.

❹ Sant'Andrea delle Fratte The bizarre shapes of the tower and cupola of this church, rebuilt by Borromini, are striking. Inside, the two angels near the choir are the originals made by Bernini for the Ponte Sant'Angelo and were replaced on the bridge by copies. They hold two instruments of the Passion.

❺ Fontana di Trevi One of the greatest attractions for tourists is this fountain by Nicola Salvi. Fed by an ancient water pipe, the fountain is flamboyantly baroque not only in its decoration but also in its use of the playing waters.

❻ Piazza Colonna This square is named after the column glorifying Emperor Marcus Aurelius. To its north is the Palazzo Chigi, the official seat of the Italian prime minister, and to its west stands the neoclassical Palazzo Wedekind, with its impressive façade of ancient columns. Reliefs on the Colonna di Marco Aurelio show Roman victories. The crowning statue of St Paul was added in 1589, replacing one of the emperor, which had long disappeared.

❼ Sant'Ignazio This Jesuit church dedicated to St Ignatius of Loyola was built between 1626 and 1680. It has impressive trompe l'oeil ceiling paintings by Andrea Pozzo, which

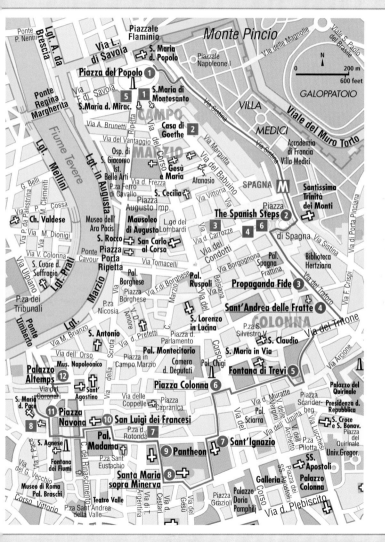

Ponte P. Nenni
Lgt. A. da Brescia
Via L. di Savoia
Piazzale Flaminio
Monte Pincio
Viale delle Magnolie
Viale di S. Paolo del Brasile

Piazza del Popolo 1
S. Maria d. Popolo
Piazzale Napoleone I
N
0   200 m
600 feet

Via F. di Savoia
5 1
S.Maria di Montesanto
S.Maria d. Mirac.
CAMPO
VILLA
MEDICI
Viale del Muro Torto
GALOPPATOIO

Ponte Regina Margherita
Via
Ripetta
Via del Corso
Via Sistina
Casa di Goethe 2
MARZIO
Via Margutta
Accademia di Francia Villa Medici

Fiume Tevere
Lgt. in Augusta
Mellini
G. Belli
M. Clementi
Cossa
Via A. Brunetti
Via del Vantaggio
Osp. di S. Giacomo
Ist. Belle Arti
P.za Ferro e Cavallo
Via d. Frezza
Gesù e Maria
Via del Babuino
Atanasio
Via Vittoria
SPAGNA M
Santissima Trinità dei Monti

Via P. da Palestrina
Via M. Dionigi
Via V. Colonna
Museo dell' Ara Pacis
Mausoleo di Augusto
Piazza Augusto Imp.
L.go dei Lombardi
S. Cecilia
Piazza di Spagna
The Spanish Steps 2
6
4
3
Via d. Carrozze
Via Sistina
Via di Porta Pinciana

S. Cuore d. Suffragio
Lgt. Prati
S. Rocco
San Carlo al Corso
Ponte Cavour
Piazza Porta Ripetta
Via Tomacelli
Via dei Condotti
Pal. Spagna
Frattina
Biblioteca Hertziana
Via F. Crispi
Via del Tritone

Via Ulpiano
Lgt. Marzio
Pal. Borghese
P.za Borghese
Via Fdi Borghese
Via d. Amore
Pal. Ruspoli
Via Borgognona
Via della Bocca
Propaganda Fide 3
Sant'Andrea delle Fratte 4

P.za dei Tribunali
Ponte Umberto
P.za Nicosia
Via M. Brianzo
Via d. Scrofa
Via d. Prefetti
S. Lorenzo in Lucina
Piazza d. Parlamento
P.za S. Silvestro
S. Claudio
COLONNA
Via del Tritone

S. Antonio
Via dell' Orso
Mus. Napoleonico
Pal. Montecitorio
Piazza in Campo Marzio
Camera d. Deputati
Pal. Chigi
S. Maria in Via
Fontana di Trevi 5
Via Arcione

Palazzo Altemps 12
Via dei Coronari
Sant' Agostino
Via delle Coppelle
Piazza Capranica
Piazza Colonna 6
Via d. Muratte
Via delle Vergini
Pal. Sciarra
Piazza Scanderbeg
Palazzo del Quirinale
Presidenza della Repubblica

S. Maria d. Pace
11 **Piazza Navona**
10 **San Luigi dei Francesi**
7
P.za di Rotonda
Via d. Umiltà
Via Lucchesi
S. Croce e S. Bonav.
Piazza del Quirinale
Univ. Gregor.

S. Agnese
Pal. **Madama**
P.za Sant Eustachio
9 **Pantheon**
7 **Sant'Ignazio**
SS. **Apostoli**

Fontana dei Fiumi
Museo di Roma Pal. Braschi
C. del Rinascimento
Teatro Valle
Santa Maria sopra Minerva 8
Via di S. Cesarini
Via del Gesù
Piazza Grazioli
Palazzo Doria Pamphilj
Galleria Colonna
Palazzo **Colonna**
P.za della Pilotta

Corso Vittorio
P.za Sant Andrea della Valle
Piazza di T. Argentina
Via d. Plebiscito
Corso

The Piazza della Rotonda is overshadowed by the Pantheon.

increase the spatial perspective, fake a cupola, and blur the boundaries between architecture, sculpture, and painting. A marble circle in the floor shows the best place to stand to enjoy the effect.

8 **Santa Maria sopra Minerva** This Gothic Dominican church, built in the 13th century over an ancient temple to Minerva, and altered in the 19th century, contains frescoes by Filippino Lippi and Michelangelo's statue *The Redeemer* (c. 1520). The *Elefantino* in front of the church is the famous sculpture of an elephant supporting an obelisk by Gian Lorenzo Bernini.

9 **Pantheon** Formerly a temple to all gods, this building owes its excellent state of preservation to its conversion into a Christian church. Originally constructed under Augustus, the Pantheon gained its circular form during the reign of Hadrian, topped by a dome symbolizing the heavens, the home of the gods. The classic proportion of 1:1 used for the diameter and interior height of the dome (43.2 m/142 ft) is perfection in architectural terms.

10 **San Luigi dei Francesi** The French national church is famous for its paintings by Caravaggio – the *Calling of St Matthew*, *The Inspiration of St Matthew*, and the *Martyrdom of St Matthew*.

11 **Piazza Navona** An elongated oval built over the outline of an ancient stadium, the Piazza Navona has three fountains, including Bernini's *Fountain of the Four Rivers* (Danube, Nile, Ganges, and Rio de la Plata). Beyond it extend the baroque church Sant'Agnese in Agone and the Palazzo Pamphili.

12 **Palazzo Altemps** Past the Renaissance church of Santa Maria della Pace, with its famous baroque façade by Pietro da Cortona and interior frescoes by Raphael, you arrive at the Palazzo Altemps, now home to a branch of the Museo Nazionale Romano.

SHOPPING

1 **Borsalino** Makers of top-quality hats for 150 years. A genuine Borsalino is an ideal choice to cut a dash on the streets of Rome for artists and politicians – not to mention gangsters.
Piazza del Popolo 20,
Tel 06 32 65 08 38,
www.borsalino.com,
siehe Via Condotti.

2 **Elio Ferraro** In the Via Margutta and adjacent streets, you're in the right place for antiques, furniture, and designer

Caffè Greco – Goethe, Liszt, and Casanova were amogn the celebrities who've enjoyed a coffee here over the centuries.

items. Elio Ferraro runs a shop of 1960s-style furniture, accessories, and vintage designer clothing.
Via Margutta 11,
www.elioferraro.com,
Mon–Sat 9.30–19.30.

3 Via Condotti With the Spanish Steps always in view, the Via Condotti is the ultimate in stylish shopping streets. Chic Roman women and elegant Roman men come here to (window-)shop in the Armani, Gucci, Beltrami, and Ferragamo stores.
9.00–13.00, 15.30–19.30,
daily, (16.00–20.00 in
summer).

4 Bulgari Bulgari is the number one address for sophisticated jewelry design in Rome, the equal of famous brands like Tiffany & Co. in New York and Cartier in Paris. The shop itself is chic and elegant.

Via dei Condotti 10,
Tel 06 679 38 76,
www.bulgari.com,
siehe Via Condotti.

EATING AND DRINKING

5 Dal Bolognese Romans, politicians, and tourists who have reserved in advance can enjoy pappardelle pasta with duck ragout, grilled fish or the house special, bollito misto, different cooked meats served with salsa verde.
Piazza del Popolo 1–2,
Tel 06 361 14 26,
Tues–Sun 12.45–15.00,
20.15–23.00.

6 Caffè Greco Goethe, Byron, Wagner, and Bizet, to name but a few, all enjoyed drinking their coffee here. Busts and portraits are a reminder of former famous guests and owners, and maintain the aura of former times.

Via Condotti 86,
Tel 06 79 17 00,
Mon–Sat 8.00–20.45.

7 Tazza d'Oro Reputedly the best cappuccino in the city, though unfortunately there is no seating. Order *un cappuccino da portar via* and enjoy the wonderful aroma.
Via degli Orfani 84,
Tel 06 678 97 92,
www.tazzadorocoffeeshop.
com, Mon–Sun 7.00–20.00.

8 Antico Caffè della Pace Near the church of Santa Maria della Pace, this coffee shop has been a popular meeting place since 1891. Enjoy a coffee in the beautiful interior, richly decorated with antiques and paintings, or outside the ivy-clad building.
Via della Pace 3–7,
Tel 06 686 12 16,
www.caffedellapace.it,
9.00–2.00, daily.

Castel Sant'Angelo and Ponte Sant'Angelo with its romantic night-time illuminations.

SIGHTS

1 Il Gesù The design of Il Gesù, mother church of the Jesuit Order, built in 1551–1584, was revolutionary at the time: the façade and interior influenced many later baroque churches. The decoration of the interior and the ceiling fresco, the *Triumph of the Name of Jesus* by Baciccia, date from the high baroque period, and the marble cladding in the nave is 19th century. In the left transept, the altar over the tomb of St Ignatius, designed by Andrea Pozzo and decorated with lapis lazuli columns, is worthy of particular attention.

2 Sant'Andrea della Valle The mother church of the Counter-Reformation Theatine Order, founded by St Cajetan, is stylistically an early baroque structure, built in the first half of the 17th century. The façade

has a more upright and dynamic effect than that of Il Gesù, but the interior appears to be less severe. Look out for the frescoes by Giovanni Lanfranco, Domenichino, and Mattia Preti. The Cappella Attavanti on the right of the nave was the setting for Act 1 of Puccini's *Tosca*.

3 Campo de' Fiori Every morning, one of the largest and most picturesque markets in Rome takes place here around the memorial to Giordano Bruno, the Dominican monk who left the "correct" path and was burned at the stake here as a heretic in 1600. At night the area is very lively.

4 Palazzo Farnese The most important high Renaissance palace in Rome, now home to the French Embassy and nicknamed "dado" (the Cube), has an impressive design by the

master architects Antonio da Sangallo the Younger and Michelangelo.

5 Cancelleria Another very important city palace, built between 1489 and 1513; it still displays the typical features

of the early Renaissance when compared with the Palazzo Farnese.

6 Chiesa Nuova The church of Santa Maria in Vallicella has a miraculous painting of the Madonna, framed by paintings by Peter Paul Rubens. The stunning frescoes in the baroque church are the work of Pietro da Cortona. The front façade of the adjacent Oratorio dei Filippini (oratory of St Philip Neri) is even more spectacular, its beautifully curved shapes having been designed by Francesco Borromini.

7 Castel Sant'Angelo and Ponte Sant'Angelo The angels on the bridge carry the instruments of the Passion of Christ and were produced by

Santa Maria in Trastevere is the main landmark in the Trastevere district of Rome.

Bernini's pupils, according to his designs. The Castel Sant'Angelo, once the tomb of Roman emperors from Hadrian to Caracalla, then a papal refuge, is today a museum

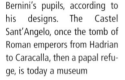 **St Peter's Basilica** Built as a centrally planned church on a Greek cross to plans by Bramante and Michelangelo from 1506, then lengthened as a longitudinal church and given a façade and square by Maderno and Bernini, the basilica's interior is home to a wealth of famous works of art, including masterpieces by Bernini and the *Pietà* by Michelangelo. From the dome, there is a wonderful view over much of the city.

Camposanto Teutonico To the south of St Peter's, the German cemetery, which dates back to around the year 800, has a large number of tombs of German artists, scientists, and well-known figures.

Santa Maria in Trastevere The oldest church to the Virgin in Rome, a medieval structure from the 12th century, is famed for its mosaics. The exterior mosaic on the façade shows Mary and saints; in the interior, the mosaic in the apse shows her on a throne next to Jesus (12th C.). Below this are scenes from her life by Pietro Cavallini (1291). The area around Santa Maria, with its narrow alleyways, is a fashionable district.

San Pietro in Montorio Within the Franciscan church is Bernini's Cappella Raimondi, and in its courtyard is the famous *Tempietto* by Bramante. This is considered the most perfect structure of the high Renaissance, its shapes and proportions inspired by the lines of an ancient temple. Legend has it that it was built over the place where St Peter was crucified.

SHOPPING

Campo de' Fiori This square has one of the most beautiful markets in the city, with stalls spread out around the statue of the heretic Giordano Bruno. There's a wide range of fresh fruit and vegetables, and the fresh fish is also an attraction for locals and tourists. Unfortunately, its great popularity is also reflected in its prices.
Mon–Sat 8.00–13.30.

Spazio Sette Situated on three floors of a building behind the façade of a Renaissance palace, this is the best address in Rome for household goods, furniture, and general designer items. Beautiful items

The Campo de' Fiori is a picturesque market in the daytime and a lively and trendy gathering place at night.

in beautiful surroundings and perhaps even at beautiful prices, for yourself or as gifts.
Via dei Barbieri 7,
Tel 06 68 80 42 61,
Mon 15.30–19.30, Tues–Sat
9.30–13.00, 15.30–19.30.

3 **Officina Profumo-Farmaceutica di Santa Maria Novella** Step into this shop and be greeted by a wonderful scent of herbs and flowers. The Roman branch of the well-known Florentine pharmacy (Via della Scala 16, Florence) sells plant-based cosmetics made to the old recipes of the Dominican monks.
Corso del Rinascimento 47,
Tel 06 687 96 08,
Mon–Sat 9.30–19.30.

4 **Almost Corner Bookshop** This shop has a good selection of English-language books, with a huge assortment of bestsellers and rare titles.

Via del Moro 45,
Tel 06 583 69 42,
Mon–Sat 10.00–13.30,
15.30–20.00, Sun 11.00–13.30,
15.30–20.00.

EATING AND DRINKING

5 **Grappolo d'Oro Zampanò** This timeless trattoria close to the Campo de' Fiori offers delicious dishes, including a good selection of antipasti, salami, and formaggi (cheeses, as well as different risotti and dolci (sweets).
Piazza della Cancelleria
80–84, Tel 06 689 70 80,
www.grappolodoro
zampano.it,
in season, 12.00–15.00,
19.30–23.00, daily.

6 **Il Mozzicone** A simple and plain but very pleasant restaurant. After a visit to the Vatican, settle yourself into one of the chairs outside, relax

and fortify yourself here in more worldly style.
Via Borgo Pio 180,
Tel 06 686 15 00, Mon–Sat
12.00–15.00, 19.30–23.00.

7 **Enoteca Ferrara** One of the best restaurants in Trastevere, extending over three floors. The wine cellar contains over 20,000 bottles, offering a choice of over 1,000 wines.
Via del Moro 1/Piazza Trilussa
41, Tel 06 58 33 39 20,
www.enotecaferrara.it,
wine bar: 18.00–2.00, daily;
restaurant: 19.30– 1.00, daily.

8 **Enoteca Reggio** This simple wine bar is a great place to meet either during the day or the evening; people-watch in the piazza and chat over a glass of wine or an aperitif. The menu is fairly short, but there's a good selection of fine wine by the glass.
Piazza Campo de' Fiori 1.

Santa Maria Maggiore: each year people celebrate the miracle of its existence, with white flower petals being dropped from the ceiling.

SIGHTS

❶ San Giovanni in Laterano
The seat of the pope in his role as the bishop of Rome, this is the oldest and most high-ranking of all Roman Catholic churches. The core of the early Christian building dates back to the time of the emperor Constantine, but its current look is the result of a baroque redesign by Francesco Borromini, and changes made in the 19th century. The medieval cloister is worth a visit. Part of the baptistery next to the church also dates back to early Christian times. The adjacent Lateran Palace was the papal residence until 1308; the present building was completed in 1589.

❷ Scala Santa In a building opposite the Lateran Palace, the holy stairs are said to come from the palace of Pilate and

therefore to be the very ones climbed by Christ. They were brought to Rome by St Helena, the mother of Christian Emperor Constantine.

❸ San Clemente The church of San Clemente is built on the site of earlier structures – a Roman palace with a Mithraic temple, and a later Christian basilica. The Christian basilica is the lower church on this site, with early medieval frescoes. The upper church was built around 1100 and, in addition to beautiful Cosmatesque work and mosaics, has an important series of frescoes from the early Renaissance, with scenes from the life of St Catherine and St Ambrose by Masolino and Masaccio.

❹ San Pietro in Vincoli The most famous piece in this church, named after the chains (vincoli) in which Peter was

restrained, is the tomb for Pope Julius II by Michelangelo with its statue of Moses (1513–16).

❺ Santa Maria Maggiore
According to legend, this pilgrim church was built in the 5th century on a site where snow fell in August. Much modified over the centuries, the interior is mainly baroque, but the colonnades and the mosaics high on the wall and on the triumphal arch in front of the choir date from the time of its construction in 432.

❻ Museo Nazionale Romano
This museum at the Baths of Diocletian houses a collection of ancient statues, mosaics, and paintings; its rooms give an impression of the size of the former imperial baths complex.

❼ Santa Maria degli Angeli
One of the most unusual basilicas in Rome; it was designed

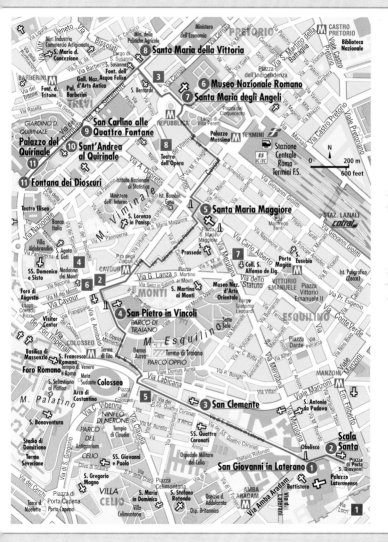

Min. Industria
Commercio Artigianato
S. Maria di
Concezione

8 Santa Maria della Vittoria

6 Museo Nazionale Romano

7 Santa Maria degli Angeli

Pal. d'Arte Antica

San Carlino alle
9 Quattro Fontane

Palazzo del
Quirinale
10 Sant'Andrea
al Quirinale

11 Fontana dei Dioscuri

5 Santa Maria Maggiore

S. Lorenzo
in Panisp.

S. Prassede

7 Coll. S.
Alfonso de Lig.

Porta
Magica

S. Eusebio

Museo Naz.
d'Arte
Orientale

4 San Pietro in Vincoli

Visitor
Center

Basilica di
Massenzio

Foro Romano

Colosseo

5

3 San Clemente

S. Antonio
da Padova

Scala
Santa

2

Obelisco

San Giovanni in Laterano **1**

Battistero

Palazzo
Lateranense

Stazione
Centrale
Roma –
Termini F.S.

N

0   200 m
0   600 feet

The Santa Maria degli Angeli Basilica was built on the site of an earlier building, like many other structures in Rome.

in about 1560 by Michelangelo, who integrated it into a section of the ancient Baths of Diocletian. Inside the church, the enormous scale of the room, the former tepidarium, as well as ancient columns betrays its former function.

8 Santa Maria della Vittoria This small baroque church is home to the Cappella Cornaro (1646) by Gianlorenzo Bernini in which St Teresa of Avila, a 16th-century Spanish mystic, has her heart pierced by an angel. Members of the Venetian family Cornaro watch, as if in auditorium boxes. Bernini created this extraordinary work of art that encompasses the whole chapel.

9 San Carlino alle Quattro Fontane With its façade of undulating columns (1662) and an almost completely white interior (1634) with complex architectural devices, this church by Francesco Borromini is a high point of Roman baroque architecture.

10 Sant'Andrea al Quirinale Built by Bernini, 1658–70, this remarkable church building is oval in shape and positioned sideways, a solution forced on Bernini by the shape of the site itself. On entering, you are immediately aware of the proximity of the altar to the entrance. The church was once intended for the Jesuit novitiate, but it later became the court church of Italian royalty.

11 Palazzo del Quirinale and the Fontana dei Dioscuri Originally the summer residence of the popes, then the palace of the Italian kings, this palazzo is today the residence of the Italian president. The square in front of the palace contains an Egyptian obelisk and the group of Castor and Pollux from the ancient baths of the emperor Constantine.

SHOPPING

1 Mercato di Sannio This bazaar-like street market extends along the Aurelian Walls, and has a covered section. Search here for all kinds of useful items and bric-a-brac, including both new and secondhand clothing, bags, militaria, and rather bizarrely, fishing equipment.
Via Sannio,
Mon–Fri 8.00–13.00,
Sat 8.00–16.00.

2 La Bottega del Cioccolato A magical small shop selling all manner of handmade chocolates and pralines. Its bestsellers include masks made from chocolate and Roman sights such as the Coliseum and St Peter's, also made of

The Italian president's residence is in the Palazzo del Quirinale.

chocolate – tempting edible souvenirs that might not make it back home, especially on a sweltering summer's day!
Via Leonina 82,
Tel 06 482 14 73,
www.labottegadelcioccolato.it

3 Feltrinelli International A real treasure trove for bookworms, with an enormous selection of both Italian and foreign-language books, mainly on history, art, food, and travel. There are also art prints and film posters.
Via Vittorio Emanuele
Orlando 84–86,
Tel 06 482 78 78,
Mon–Sat 9.00–20.00, Sun
10.30–3.30, 16.00–20.00.

4 Eventi Young and provocative fashion for those who prefer the avant-garde rather than simple elegance.
Via dei Serpenti 134,
Tel 06 48 49 60.

EATING AND DRINKING

5 Cannavota A traditional Italian restaurant with nostalgic décor. The antipasti are strongly recommended, as are the delicious pasta dishes, particularly the homemade cannelloni, which are fantastic. The food is very good value for money, and the service is always very attentive.
Piazza San Giovanni in
Laterano 20,
Tel 06 77 20 50 07,
Thurs–Tues 12.30–15.00,
19.30–23.00; closed Aug.

6 Leonina A much loved and very busy pizzeria – and no wonder, because these are arguably the best pizzas in Rome, sold in rectangualr slices, straight from the baking tray – you pay by weight, and the prices are not bad at all. Try the unusual roasted potatoes and rosemary pizza.

Via Leonina 84,
Tel 06 482 77 44,
7.30–22.00, daily.

7 Trattoria Monti A family-run trattoria near the Basilica Santa Maria Maggiore serving some excellent meat, chicken, and rabbit dishes. An excellent wine list as well. Reservations are required.
Via di San Vito 13 a,
Tel 06 446 65 73,
closed Sun and Mon.

8 Ristorante del Giglio This popular restaurant, located very close to the Teatro dell'Opera, is known for its excellent traditional and rustic style cooking and for its attentive service. It specializes in dishes from Rome and from the Latium region.
Via Torino 137,
Tel 06 488 16 06,
closed Sun and Mon at
midday.

INDEX

PICTURE CREDITS/IMPRINT

MONACO BOOKS is an imprint of Verlag Wolfgang Kunth
© Verlag Wolfgang Kunth GmbH & Co.KG, Munich, 2011
Concept: Wolfgang Kunth
Editing and design: Verlag Wolfgang Kunth GmbH&Co.KG
English translation/editing: Silva Editions Ltd.; JMS Books LLP

For distribution please contact:
Monaco Books
c/o Verlag Wolfgang Kunth, Königinstr.11
80539 München, Germany
Tel: +49 / 89/45 80 20 23
Fax: +49 / 89/ 45 80 20 21
info@kunth-verlag.com
www.monacobooks.com
www.kunth-verlag.de

NOTES

NOTES

NOTES

NOTES

NOTES